THE ANATOMY OF

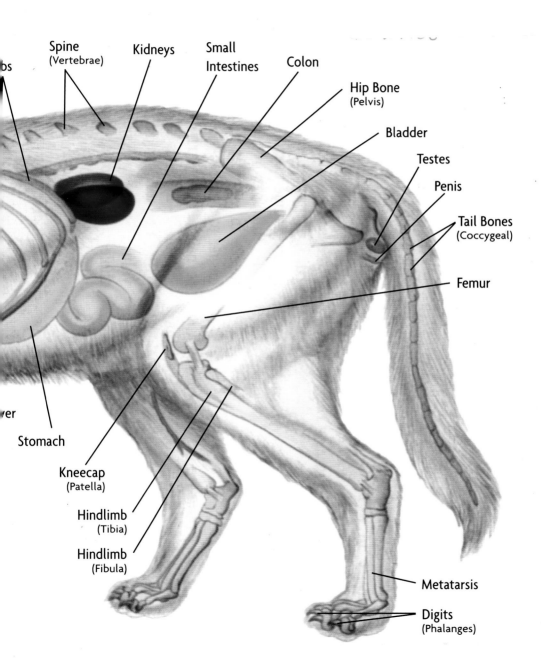

Spine
(Vertebrae)

Kidneys

Small
Intestines

Colon

Hip Bone
(Pelvis)

Bladder

Testes

Penis

Tail Bones
(Coccygeal)

Femur

bs

ver

Stomach

Kneecap
(Patella)

Hindlimb
(Tibia)

Hindlimb
(Fibula)

Metatarsis

Digits
(Phalanges)

Abyssinian Cat

◇

By Virginia N Tidwell

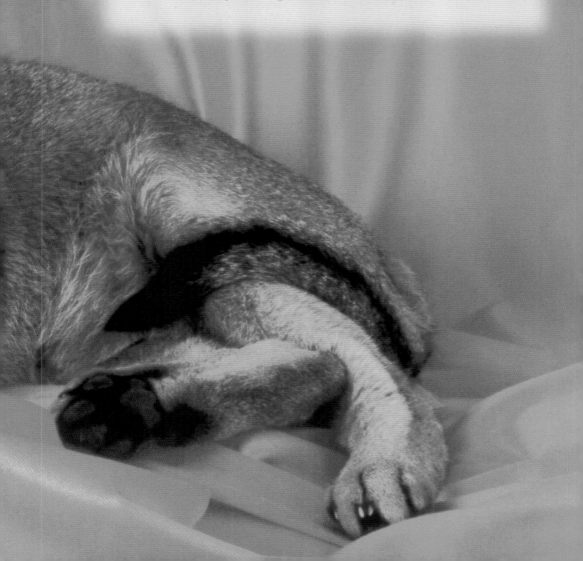

CONTENTS

PUBLISHED IN THE UNITED KINGDOM BY:

INTERPET
PUBLISHING

Vincent Lane, Dorking   Surrey RH4 3YX   England

ISBN 1-84286-045-3

PHOTO CREDITS
Photography by Isabelle Français, and Alan Robinson
with additional photographs by Animal Health Trust,
Michael W Brim, Cat Fanciers Association, Carolina Biological Supply,
Fleabusters Rx for Fleas, James R Hayden, RBP, Interpet, Dwight R Kuhn,
Dr Dennis Kunkel, Mikki Pet Products, Phototake, Jean Claude Revy,
Erin Winters and WB Saunders Company.

The publisher wishes to thank the following cat owners for allowing their
Abys to be photographed for this book: Suzanne Borowicz, Lauren Castle,
Sally L Deegan, Ada M Demmler, Denise Ogle Donahue, Kent Fleming,
Chris Giammarinaro, Meredith Gowell, Annette Kielhurn, Teresa Mitchell,
Kimberly O'Boyle, and Kathy Lyn Parrish.

History of the
ABYSSINIAN CAT

One of the fascinating attractions of the cat fancy is the mystery that surrounds the history and development of many of its breeds. No other pet hobby can quite compare with it in the romance and richness of its claims and stories. Certainly, the Abyssinian has its share of both mystery and contradictions in respect to its lineage.

The breed also has more than a few skeletons in its cupboard that destroy the popular notion that it traces back directly to the time of the Pharaohs and that show that its lineage as a 'pure' breed goes no further back in time than the 1940s.

However, putting aside occasional outcrosses to other breeds and its mixed genetic base, there is no doubt that the Abyssinian, or 'Aby,' as it is known affectionately, is indeed one of the oldest of the domestic cat breeds. This said, we must not go overboard on the matter. 'Oldest' in acceptable breed terms means having existed since the later years of the 19th century—not from the time when cats graced the temples of

Bubastis in the Nile delta nearly 3000 years ago.

The reason that the late 1800s are of importance is because, in 1871, Harrison Weir staged the world's first major cat show at the Crystal Palace in Sydenham, London. In so doing, he set in motion the cat fancy as an organised hobby, which would produce the wide range of breeds we see today.

Despite the allure of Egyptian mythology, the modern Abyssinian traces its origins only back as far as the 1940s in England.

THE FELINE GENE POOL
Prior to 1871, the only cats in Britain that could be regarded as breeds by present-day standards were the Persian, Angora, Siamese and Manx—each being based on a mutational form readily identified. All other domestic cats at that time were a mixed bag of shorthaired feline sorts in respect

to their type, colour and pattern.

Domestic cats had arrived in England over many centuries from all parts of the world. The gene pool was, therefore, exceedingly large and varied, and provided the potential to create many forms once breeders had a need to be selective in what they wanted to achieve. The emerging cat fancy provided that need.

However, in the early years of the hobby, there were no registration bodies, pedigrees were all but unheard of and there were no national breed clubs, books or cat magazines to guide would-be owners. Genetics was an unknown subject and there was no consensus about how a breed was defined. Nor were there any cat experts *per se*; everything started from the ground up.

A breed was a breed largely because a person, or a small group of people, said it was. Such people were the early pioneers who had become judges and breeders. Only later were national clubs formed. Via these clubs, concepts of breed status and origins were accepted or rejected—for better or worse, depending in which camp of thought you resided.

ABYSSINIAN ORIGIN

In the earliest years of the cat fancy, cats of similar colour or pattern often were given a wide variety of names, many of which predated the creation of the cat fancy. These varieties, whether genuinely different or merely alternative names for the same type, were interbred quite indiscriminately. Even recognised breeds, as they were developed, were hybridised. Against this background, it can therefore be stated that the Abyssinian, as we know it today, did not exist as a pure breed when the cat fancy commenced.

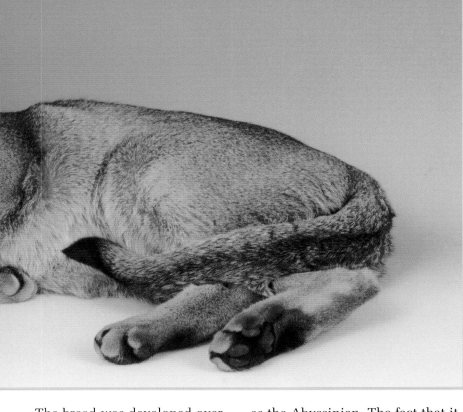

The Abyssinian breed is largely defined by its unique ticked coloration, which has been identified on a number of similarly constructed cats from ancient times. The ruddy coloration, shown here, is also referred to as the usual colour.

The breed was developed over a number of years by selective breeding from indigenous and introduced ticked cats, as well as via a degree of outcrossing to other breeds. The Abyssinian is thus as British in its origin as is the Bulldog or the Union Jack. Credit for the breed must be given fairly and squarely to the breed's pioneers, who had the vision and determination to create the wonderful feline we know today as the Abyssinian. The fact that it looks similar to the bronze cats of Egypt dating to the 7th century BC is purely because those early breeders, and the ones that followed, chose wisely in the cats that they used to pursue their objective.

It is fanciful in the extreme to harbour the notion that the Aby derives from a tribal people in some foreign land who had preserved the breed over many centuries. In one sense, the breed's pioneers were themselves responsible for this notion.

ZULA

The first specific reference to a particular cat from Abyssinia is found in *Cats: Their Points and Characteristics*, published in 1874 and written by William Gordon Staples. It states that the wife of a Captain Barret-Lennard, while in Abyssinia, acquired a female cat called Zula, which she took back to England with her following the end of the Abyssinian campaign of 1867–1868. Brian Fitzgerald, in his work *The Domestic Cat*, published in 1969, revealed, however, that the Barrett-Lennard family had no trace of either the lady or the cat in question.

However, there is no reason to doubt the existence of the cat.

The 'mother of us all,' the Persian has been used in the creation of most long-haired breeds and to improve most other breeds.

> ## THE SOMALI
> The Somali is the longhaired variety of the Abyssinian. The breed was developed in America during the early 1970s from longhaired Abyssinians that traced back to Raby Chuffa, exported from England to America in 1952. For a number of years, the Somali was the source of many angry debates, but eventually common sense prevailed and the breed gained official recognition, which it now enjoys throughout the world.
>
> The longhaired gene had probably existed in the British Aby from earlier times when the breed had been crossed to the Persian or Angora. With the passage of time, these crosses probably were forgotten. The Somali is judged against the same standard as the Abyssinian, except for its somewhat longer bodily fur and brush-like tail. It is a quite beautiful breed. Unfortunately, like the Balinese (longhaired Siamese), the Somali does not generate the support that its appearance deserves.

Zula obviously was named after the makeshift port of that name, used as the place of debarkation for a 13,000-strong Anglo-Indian force that the British sent to Abyssinia from Bombay under the command of Sir Robert Napier in 1867. Following their victory in the battle of Arogi, the British

Developed in America during a period when long hair was quite the rage, the Somali hails back to the early 1970s. Although never as popular as its sleek-haired Abyssinian brother, the Somali has gained a following around the world.

WHAT'S IN A NAME?

The name Abyssinian, as applied to a specific type, came into use only about 1882, when cats were entered as Abyssinian at the Crystal Palace Show. However, it was known that ticked cats existed in Abyssinia (now Ethiopia and Eritrea in Northeast Africa) from earlier times.

Other names applied to sub-varieties of the ticked tabby were Russian, Spanish, British Ticked, Hare Cat, Cunny, Bunny Cat and Rabbit Cat—some even believed that ticked cats were the result of a cross between a rabbit and a cat! The name Bunny Cat, in particular, persisted alongside that of Abyssinian into the 1920s.

Specific breed names slowly became established on the premise that a breed that had an exotic-sounding name and lineage had a much better chance of eliciting interest and support than one that did not. The cat fancy was very much the domain of the middle and upper classes. Once the hobby was well underway, any suggestion that a breed was of 'common' moggie origin was quickly shed. All attempts were made to focus ancestry on some distant place, where the breed was supposedly held in the greatest of esteem and was highly valued. Such cats would have greater value than moggies.

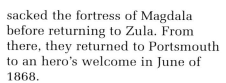

As it was known that ticked cats had been brought to England from Abyssinia in the years that preceded the first cat show, this fact no doubt helped the future linking of the breed's name to a ticked variety. One such import, Zula, was to be recorded—the only one as far as is known that was actually documented.

sacked the fortress of Magdala before returning to Zula. From there, they returned to Portsmouth to an hero's welcome in June of 1868.

Zula the cat was portrayed lying on a cushion in a lithograph featured in the book. However, she hardly could be regarded as being an example of the Abyssinian unless she was viewed through rose-tinted spectacles! She had a round full-cheeked face, very short ears, a stocky body and no suggestion of tabby markings on her legs, neck or face.

This may, however, indicate a poor artist. After her moment of fame, she was never heard of again.

Interestingly, Zula was described as being quite wild when first acquired, this suggesting she was a feral or wholly wild feline. However, her importance to the Abyssinian is that she appeared in the book. This may well have been the cat that prompted the eventual strong association of ticked cats with the then in-vogue country of Abyssinia.

HARRISON WEIR

In 1889, Harrison Weir's book *Our Cats and All About Them* was published. In this most influential work, his comments on the Aby were illuminating. At that time, the Aby still was not believed by most experts to be other than a variety of the common tabby, so it is worthwhile quoting Weir.

He, too, felt that the Aby was no different, other than in colour, from the ordinary tabby cat of which it was a variety. But later he states, 'Still several have been imported from Abyssinia, all of which were precisely similar.' He also states, 'The imported cats are of a stouter build than the English and less marked.'

In the section on breeding Abyssinians, he says, 'To breed these true, it is well to procure imported stock or pedigree stock, for many cats are bred in England from ordinary tabbies that so nearly resemble the Abyssinian in colour as scarcely to be distinguished from the much-prized foreigners.'

Under 'Abyssinian Crosses' he states, 'Curiously coloured as the Abyssinian cat is, and being a true breed, no doubt of long far back ancestry...' This is in complete contradiction to his comments about the breed's being a mere variety of the English ticked. He also suggests that it makes a fine cross with the Persian, Russian, Angora or Archangel breed. No doubt this advice was taken by some and may account for the longhaired gene in the Aby, as well as the introduction of various colours.

In the same book, Mr Weir gives the first standard for the Aby (which he drafted). This is surprisingly well done (give or take a few oddities), as are all other standards in the book. Indeed, Weir created the blueprint for the way standards should be

THE CRYSTAL PALACE SHOW

On 13 July 1871, an event took place that changed the world of the domestic cat. In the Crystal Palace at Sydenham, London, the world's first all-breed cat show took place. It was organised by Harrison Weir (1824–1906), a noted animal artist and great lover of British Shorthairs.

The success of the cat show saw Weir become a noted cat judge and author. Today he is regarded as the 'father of the cat fancy.' The Crystal Palace show attracted thousands of people, many of whom had never seen, or were not even aware of, some of the breed types. On display were many British Shorthairs, Siamese, Manx and a wild cat.

prepared. His method remains the one still in use by all major cat registries.

PROBLEMS AND PIONEERS

In spite of the exposure given to the Aby by Weir in his book, the breed remained very much a rarity in the cat fancy. To compound matters, a silver ticked variety, mentioned by Weir, became popular. A negative offspin of this was that, when crossed with the traditional rufous red colour, the subsequent undercoat of the red became degraded to a greyish colour. This added to the controversy surrounding the breed.

Early authorities, such as H C Brooke and Captain W H Powell, were horrified at the damage done by the silvers to the developing breed. They stated that silver was totally alien to the Abyssinian. They would no doubt have been horrified if they saw the colours now accepted in the breed!

In 1887, the National Cat Club was formed and, in 1896, it issued its first stud book. In it, just two Abyssinians appeared—Sedgemere Bottle (born 1892) and Sedgemere Peaty (born 1894). In both instances, their parents were unknown. In the following years, a number of well-known cats had one of their parents marked as unknown. These included Fancy Free 1903 (bred by Mrs Carew-Cox) Cojam 1906 (also bred by

Mrs Carew-Cox) and Silver Memelik 1907 (bred by Lady Deices).

The leading sires at the turn of the century were Aluminium 1905 and Ras Dashan 1908. Both were bred by Mrs Carew-Cox, whose original pair of Abys were given to her and of unknown origin. Interestingly, Mrs Carew-Cox, apart from being pre-eminent in the Abyssinian, was also at that time equally as well known for being involved in developing the Russian Blue.

Mrs Carew-Cox had an enormous influence on the Abyssinian, and H C Brooke felt that, following his own retire-ment, the Aby might well have vanished were it not for her efforts and enthusiasm.

To add to the problems of the Aby, as the century came to a close, a second feline club and registry, the Cat Club, came into being in 1898. This created divisions in the hobby. A consequence of the rivalry was that the Cat Club dropped the name Abyssinian in favour of the name Ticked. This no doubt continued to fuel the confusion in respect to the Abyssinian.

THE BREED PROGRESSES

In 1910, following more problems between clubs, the Governing Council of the Cat Fancy (GCCF) was formed. This unified the hobby. The term Abyssinian had emerged as the single name for any tick-patterned cat, though the name Bunny Cat lingered on. There were now only six recognised cat breeds in Britain: the Persian, Siamese, British Shorthair, Manx, Russian Blue and Abyssinian.

With a rather difficult history behind it, today's Abyssinian is a gorgeous feline that shimmers with purity and a style all its own.

As a guide to its rarity (or lofty status) in 1912, a pair of Aby show kittens were selling for about £5.5 shillings, compared to the £1.1 shilling for a pair of Russian Blues or British Shorthairs. As the century progressed, the fortunes of the breed improved somewhat, especially after the formation of the Abyssinian Cat Club in 1929.

Many breeders were becoming well established and famous around this time. Among these were Lady Liverpool (Merkland), Major Sydney Woodiwiss (Woodroofe), Lady Barnard (Raby) and Mrs Clare Basnet (Croham). These breeders would provide many of the cats that commenced the breed in Europe and America.

The Aby failed to ignite enthusiasm in America during the turn-of-the-century years but, in 1934, fresh imports resulted in the breed's establishment. After a slow start, the breed went on to become, as it remains, enormously popular in that country. It is thought that the first Abys were imported into France during 1927, into Denmark during 1950 and into Australia in 1959. The breed is now well established throughout Europe.

WORLD WAR II

Just when things appeared to be really progressing, the Second World War commenced. This had a devastating effect on all cat breeds, and especially so on the Abyssinian, whose numbers already were small. It is thought that when hostilities ended in 1945, there may have been about only 12 Abys left in Britain. Fortunately, breeders were able to import stock that was developed from British lines from America and Europe. Even so, it was an uphill task to re-establish the breed.

Outcrosses to other breeds were necessary in order to keep the gene pool viable. These breeds were the British Shorthair, the Siamese, possibly the Burmese and maybe also the Russian Blue, which was not in good shape itself in respect to numbers.

By the 1950s, the Abyssinian was attracting a flow of new and enthusiastic breeders. Of these, Florence Bone (Nigella) and Edith Menezes (Taisham) are but two of many whose skills after the war helped re-established the Abyssinian.

In Europe, during 1990 in Munich, the FIFe (Federation Internationale Feline) organised a World Show that has become an annual event. At this prestigious exhibition, the Abyssinian has attained many World Winner titles. In Britain, at the 20th annual Supreme Show of the GCCF in 1996, an Abyssinian Grand Champion, Mikkar Giddy Kipper, became the first Aby to win the much-coveted Supreme Adult award. This was a fitting testimony to the Aby's resurgence

The blue Abyssinian possesses a soft warm blue coat over a pinkish mushroom undercoat. This colour is actually the dilution of the usual colour, present in the breed as early as 1891 but only recognised in Britain in 1984.

The sorrel coloration, as it is called in Britain, is referred to as red in the US and cinnamon in Australia. The author feels that the latter name is most correct, genetically speaking.

from the gloomy days that befell the breed during the war years.

THE FUTURE

The future for the Abyssinian in Britain and many other countries, other than America, is likely to remain, as it has always been, one with a difficult battle for survival. It is neither a flashy breed nor one likely to suddenly become fashionable. But as long as there are those in the cat fancy who appreciate the finer points of quality within a domestic feline, the breed's future is secure. The Aby has always been, and remains, a connoisseur's choice.

From the potential owner's viewpoint, one major advantage of a less popular breed is that the general standard of quality with the breed is normally much higher than is the case within very popular breeds. Even the typical pet-quality Abyssinian kitten still will be a fine feline. If you are thinking of becoming a breeder and want to make lots of spare cash, forget the Aby. But if you want to really feel part of a breed, there are a lot of devoted enthusiasts waiting to help you achieve that end in a breed that truly is quite exquisite.

All the world agrees that the Aby is one fine-looking animal, prized for its natural beauty and harmonious appearance.

Portrait of the
ABYSSINIAN CAT

Beauty is a quality not easily described, because what one person sees as beautiful may be regarded as an abomination by someone else. This said, it is doubtful that you could find any true cat lover that did not agree that the Abyssinian was at the least a very fine-looking breed, and at best an excellent example of what a structurally well-balanced feline should look like.

There is no exaggeration about the Abyssinian. It is not svelte like the Siamese, cobby like the British Shorthair or built like the feline equivalent of a Bulldog. It is a truly elegant cat. The same comment can be made about its coat pattern. It is not a pattern that dazzles those unfamiliar with cat breeds. Yet, its very simplicity blends perfectly with the breed's external form to create a cat that is at one with the concept of what a natural breed should look like.

THE BREED STANDARD

A breed standard is a document that attempts to describe a theoretically ideal example of a breed, yet in such a way that it allows for differences between individual cats. One person or a group of people (usually a group of enthusiasts) drafts the standard when a cat type begins its long road towards breed status. The drafted document is presented to a feline registry for adoption. If it meets the registry's criteria, the breed is given recognition. However, it often will be some time before the new breed attains championship status, depending on the rules of a given registry. Once accepted, the standard is the yardstick by which judges and breeders alike determine quality.

A standard is not immutable. If the need arises, it can be revised by the breed's national club to reflect any needs within the breed over any given time span. The very flexibility of a standard means that it is open to considerable interpretation by breeders and judges. This is why breeds may change in their appearance—sometimes dramatically—over the years.

The Abyssinian has remained a remarkably stable breed in relation to its original standard regarding its conformation, though not its colours, depending on the registry under consideration. Breed standards differ to varying degrees among the registries of different countries, and even among different registries within the same country. This is unfortunate, but one of the realities of the cat fancy.

In Britain, mainland Europe and Australia, colour in the Aby is always allocated more points than is the case in American registries. Differences in certain aspects of conformation, and of the coat pattern, are such that a cat in one country might lose points for a feature that would be regarded as desirable in another.

The very flexibility of a standard does mean that, to those unfamiliar with the breed, it appears a rather vague document. A standard is full of relative terms, such as *set wide apart*, *large*, *moderate* or *slight*. The only way an appreciation of these terms can be gained is by viewing many examples of the breed at cat shows. Once an understanding of what constitutes quality is gained, then recognising mediocrity becomes automatic.

The head is of a moderate wedge shape when viewed from the front.

BREED DESCRIPTION
The following breed description is not that of any one feline registry, but has been prepared after comparing those of six registries. The most well-known of these are the GCCF of Britain, the FIFe of Europe and the Cat Fanciers

Association (CFA) of America. Where deemed appropriate, hobby terms are explained.

The description should meet the needs of most potential owners. Those planning to become breeders and/or exhibitors should obtain the standard of the association with which their cats are registered.

HEAD
The head is of foreign type, meaning that it is wedge-shaped when viewed from the front. However, the wedge is nothing as extreme as seen in the Siamese. It is moderate and gently rounded. In profile, the head is again gently rounded and continues into an elegantly arched neck.

In profile, there should be a slight nose break, meaning that the line of the nose should curve gently upward into the forehead. A definite stop (indentation) or nose break (a sudden change in angles) is a fault. The muzzle is created by a slight indentation behind the whisker pads. This should not be a sharp pinch.

The chin must be firm and a theoretical line from the tip of the nose to the chin should be straight. If the upper jaw extends in front of the chin, this is known as being overshot—the incisor teeth overlap those of the lower jaw. If the chin extends in front of the upper jaw, this is called undershot. A firm chin will result in the incisor teeth of both jaws just touching, which is the correct dental bite.

EYES

The eyes should be large, set well apart and almond shaped. They are described in most standards as neither round nor Oriental. In the GCCF standard, the description is a rounded, almond shape in an Oriental setting, which means a slight slant towards the ears. All standards require the eyes to be bright and expressive

EYE COLOUR

Amber, hazel or green is the required eye colour in all standards except that of the CFA, which requires either gold or green. The colour should be as intense and deep as possible.

EARS

When viewed from the front, the outer edge of the ears should follow the line of the wedge. The ears are large, set wide apart, moderately pointed, well cupped at their base and carrying hairs on their inner edges. It is preferred that the ear tips display lynx-like tufts.

BODY

The body should be lithe, without being svelte like the Siamese. It is of medium length and bone, and should be muscular. The rib cage is rounded and should not display any suggestion of being flat-sided. The GCCF requires the back to be straight from the shoulder to the rump. The CFA, FIFe and Australian standards make no comment on this aspect, while three other of the American registries require a slightly arched back when the cat is standing.

LEGS AND PAWS

The legs should be long, relatively fine boned and elegant. Their

The Aby's eyes should be large, set well apart and almond in shape.

length should be in proportion to the body, which is carried well off the ground as would befit a tireless runner. The paws are small, compact and oval. There should be five toes on the front legs (one being the dewclaw) and four on the hind legs.

TAIL
The base of the tail is thick and the tail then tapers to a rounded tip. Its length is such that it should reach the cat's shoulders.

COAT
The standards are variable on the coat, those of the largest registries being very brief, while those of the smaller associations are more detailed. The GCCF requires a short, close-lying, fine but not soft coat. The FIFe has the same requirement but makes no comment on softness. The CFA requires a soft, silky and fine-textured coat that should be dense and resilient, carrying a lustrous sheen. Hair length is required to be medium.

The American Cat Fanciers Association (ACFA), the Cat Fanciers Federation (CFF) and the American Association of Cat Enthusiasts (AACE) have broadly similar standards, each giving the novice a better guide to the specifics of the breed's coat. That of the ACFA is typical and given here:

'Dense and resilient to the

touch, has lustrous sheen and is fine in texture. When thumbed backward it should snap back into place. The coat lies fairly close to the body, but the undercoat should be adequate enough to avoid any evidence of

The tail on the Abyssinian is thick and tapered, and capable of reaching the shoulders in length.

slickness. The coat is longest on the spine, gradually shortening over the saddle, flanks, legs and head. Length medium, but long enough to accommodate at least four alternating light and dark coloured bands.'

The necessity to give reference to the undercoat is created by the fact that the term 'close-lying' is used in other breeds, in particular the Siamese. The Siamese lacks the somewhat more dense undercoat of the

Abyssinian, which was not the case years ago. Close-lying does not therefore mean 'slick,' as seen in the Siamese and Oriental Shorthair.

BREED FAULTS

The list of faults in the Abyssinian standards is legion compared to that of many other breeds. Listed faults within the standard of the GCCF are probably the most extensive seen in any cat breed. It reflects the desire of breeders to attain perfection, especially in the coat pattern. Faults in cats come in two categories: those that are applicable to all breeds and those applicable specifically to an individual breed. Sometimes a standard may include within the breed-specific faults those that in other registries are found among the all-breed faults.

Faults are also graded in their importance. Some result in the withholding of all awards and some in the withholding of certain awards, while others result merely in loss of points. Here only the breed-specific faults are listed and are not graded in respect of importance. Rather, they are divided between those that are anatomical and those that are in relation to the coat pattern or colour. The faults are not those of any one registry, but represent a cross-section taken from a number of associations.

CONFORMATIONAL FAULTS

Cobby or Oriental type, incorrect chin, lack of slight nose break, whip tail, pinched muzzle or lack of muzzle indentation, eyes not in slanted setting, soft or over-long or coarse coat, long narrow head or short round head, and small or pointed ears.

PATTERN-COLOUR FAULTS

White markings, such as a locket, white extending down the neck or white present anywhere other than where permissible (though undesirable) as detailed in the standard. Unbroken necklets, heavy broken necklets, lack of darker tail tip, rings on the tail and poorly defined or incorrect ticking. Fewer than four bands of hair shaft colour in adults is a fault in the GCCF standard but is not specifically cited in most other standards.

Absence of required pigmentation marks on head and around eyes in adults, heavy or broken or absence of spinal shading in adults, absence of darker hind leg markings, substantial leg barring, yellow pigment anywhere on a silver cat or lack of silver due to yellow pigment on a silver cat. Pale or muddy eye colour, ghost tabby markings on the body and legs, grey undercoat close to the skin, any black hair on a red Abyssinian, off-colour paw pads and markings on the stomach or chest.

Two of the possible colours in the breed are (top) silver and (bottom) sorrel. All Aby colours are ticked throughout, giving them the distinct look for which the breed is known.

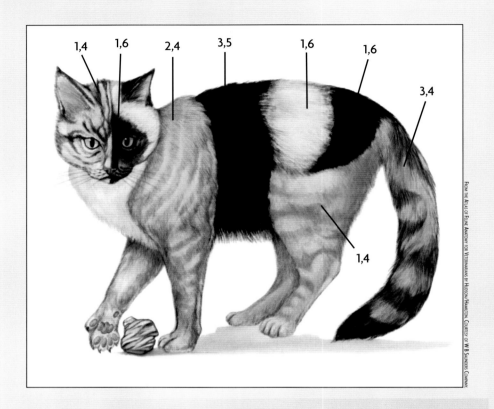

1,4   1,6   2,4   3,5   1,6   1,6   3,4   1,4

FROM THE ATLAS OF FELINE ANATOMY FOR VETERINARIANS BY HUDSON/HAMILTON. COURTESY OF W B SAUNDERS COMPANY.

PARTICOLOURED CAT

Not a new breed of feline, this 'particoloured cat' illustrates the many possibilities of the feline coat. Since cats come in three basic hair lengths, short, long and rex (curly), all three coat lengths are illustrated here. Additionally, different coat patterns, such as mackerel tabby, Abyssinian and self-coloured, are depicted to demonstrate the differences.

1–3   COAT TYPES
1 Shorthair coat
2 Rex (curly) coat
3 Longhair coat

4–6   COAT COLOUR PATTERNS
4 Mackerel (tabby)
5 Abyssinian
6 Self-coloured

SKIN AND HAIRCOAT OF CATS

Schematic illustration of histologic layers of the integument skin.

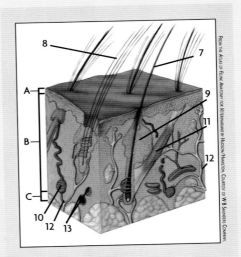

A Epidermis
B Dermis
C Subcutis

7 Primary hair
8 Secondary hairs
9 Area of sebaceous gland
10 Apocrine sweat gland
11 M arrector pili
12 Nerve fibre
13 Cutaneous vessels
14 Tactile hair
15 Fibrous capsule
16 Venous sinus
17 Sensory nerve fibres
18 External root sheath
19 Hair papilla

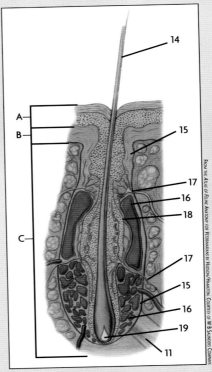

Schematic illustration of a tactile hair (whisker).

PATTERN DESCRIPTION

The ticked pattern of the Abyssinian is a modified form of the tabby pattern. However, by judicious selection, breeders over the years have endeavoured, with considerable success, to remove almost all indications of the tabby original such that the entire coat is ticked.

The general impression should be of a very well-ticked coat pattern. The minimum number of darker coloured bands required along each hair shaft varies depending on the standard under consideration. The GCCF requires three, plus a matching tip. Other associations accept a smaller number of bands. The lighter bands of colour along each hair should match the colour of the undercoat.

The eyes are highlighted by a dark line around the eyelids, this being encircled by a much lighter area of fur. There are vestigial remains of the tabby 'M' mark on the forehead, but this is indistinct. A line of the ticking colour should commence at the rear of the head and extend down the spine and along the tail before terminating as a dark tip of solid ticking colour. The same shade of ticking colour also should extend well up the hock of the hind legs.

Pigmentation lines extending from the inner edge of the eye to the top of the head, and from the outer edge of the eye to the ear,

are desirable, as are dots and shading on the whisker pads. The back of the ears should be darkest towards the tip, giving the impression of a thumbprint. It is preferred that the chest and the underparts display no markings. The chin, lips and nostrils should be the undercoat colour or cream. White or grey on these areas, and white on the throat and neck, is very undesirable. The breed's colour pattern has always proved to be the most difficult aspect to breed to the required level of quality.

SILVER PATTERN

Although the silver Aby has existed in the breed, controversially, since the breed's earliest days, it did not gain championship status until 1999 with the GCCF. The sex-linked silvers presently hold preliminary status.

The silver is created by a dominant mutation that inhibits the amount of pigment in the light-banded parts of the hair shafts. Originally, the result was a creamy white with a suffusion of yellow. Over the years, however, selective breeding has improved the colour to produce a silvery white undercoat. This is ticked with one of the standard colours, thus producing the usual silver, sorrel silver, blue silver and so on. It is a most attractive pattern and is accepted in most major registries of the world.

This handsome sorrel exhibits some white markings on its chin and neck, both of which are permitted, but not preferred.

ABYSSINIAN COLOURS

Colour	Outercoat	Undercoat	Nose Leather	Paw Pads
USUAL	Brown with black tips	Orange or apricot	Brick red	Black
BLUE	Warm blue with dark blue tips	Pinkish mushroom	Dark pink	Mauve-blue
CHOCOLATE	Copper brown with black tips	Rich apricot	Pinkish chocolate	Chocolate
SORREL	Copper with chocolate tips	Rich apricot	Rosy pink	Rosy pink
LILAC	Pinkish dove with dark tips	Pinkish cream	Mauve pink	Mauve pink
FAWN	Warm fawn or rose beige with dark tips	Fawn cream or bluish beige	Pink or salmon	Pink
RED	Warm red with darker tips	Red-apricot	Pink	Pink
CREAM	Warm cream with darker tips	Cream	Pink	Pink

By combining the silver with the tortoiseshell pattern, the tortie silver is created in its various standard colour forms. These are tortie silver, sorrel tortie silver, blue tortie silver, chocolate tortie silver, lilac tortie silver and fawn tortie silver. In each case, the silvered parts of the fur contrast with those which are non-silvered along their hair shafts.

COLOURS

With respect to colours, registries vary with regard to the number that are acceptable. Originally the breed had only one colour, but today there are eight. If these are combined with the pattern types, the potential number of combinations becomes 28. However, feline registries differ on how many of these they will accept. The GCCF accepts them all, while the CFA accepts only four.

USUAL

This is the GCCF name used for the original colour of the Abyssinian, which was described as being ruddy in the early days of the cat fancy. The term ruddy is still used in most cat registries, though in Australia it is called tawny.

The ground colour (undercoat) is a ruddy orange (burnt sienna) or apricot, while the ticking is black, though often a very dark chocolate lower down the hair shaft. The overall effect is of a rich golden brown ticked with black. The nose leather is brick red and the paw pads are black.

The blue Aby possesses dark pink nose leather and banding colours that are somewhat lighter than the hair tips.

BLUE

This is the dilution of usual and first gained recognition in Britain during 1984, though it was present in the breed as early as 1891. The overall appearance is of a soft warm blue tipped with a darker blue. As with the usual, the banding colours often are a somewhat lighter blue than the hair tip, which always must be the darkest. The undercoat is a pinkish mushroom. The nose leather is dark pink and the paw pads are a mauvish-blue.

CHOCOLATE

This is created by a mutation that reduces black to a chocolate colour, which is darkest at the hair tips. The undercoat is a rich apricot and the overall effect is of a rich copper brown tipped with chocolate. The nose leather is a pinkish chocolate and the paw pads are chocolate. This colour is still relatively new in terms of recognition, though it has been present in the breed for years.

SORREL

Created by a second mutation at the black gene locus, sorrel is a light shade of chocolate. It is called red in America and cinnamon (genetically a more correct name) in Australia. The overall effect is of a lustrous copper ticked with chocolate. The undercoat is a rich apricot (warm glowing red in America). The nose leather and paw pads are rosy pink.

The colour was originally called red in the UK (1963) but was changed to sorrel in 1979. The reason was that red in cats is a sex-linked colour and now has recognition as such in Britain, Europe and Australia, though not as yet in America. Red was present in the breed from the early days, though only specifically bred for after 1945.

LILAC

The dilution of chocolate, lilac is a warm pinkish dove, with the hair tips' being the darkest. The undercoat is a pinkish cream. The nose leather and paw pads are a mauve-pink. Like the chocolate, it is presently a new colour in respect of recognition but should, in due course, gain championship status in Britain and Europe, already having earned this status in Australia.

FAWN

The dilution of sorrel, fawn gained championship status in 2000. The hairs are banded with a warm fawn (rose-beige in America), with the hair tips' being the darkest. The undercoat is a fawn-cream (blush beige in America). The nose leather is pink, (GCCF) or salmon (CFA).The paw pads are pink with light cocoa brown between the toes. The colour, being the dilution of non-sex-linked red, is recognised internationally, including with the American registries.

Fawn coloration in the Aby is achieved by the dilution of sorrel, with hairs banded in warm fawn and a fawn-cream undercoat.

The dilution of ruddy or usual, blue has become a favourite colour among Abyssinian lovers.

RED (UK, EUROPE AND AUSTRALIA)

This is a sex-linked colour. This means the sex of the partners has a bearing on the resultant colour and pattern of the offspring. These may be red, non-red (meaning chocolate, blue, lilac and so on) or tortoiseshell, which is normally a female-only pattern. Fertile tortie males are possible, but exceedingly rare. They are the consequence of a genetic abnormality.

The tortie is created by one of the standard colours' appearing in some areas of the coat, while other areas have a lighter shade of ticking and undercoat colour. The pattern may be either random or symmetrical.

Blazes and/or solid legs and tail are all permissible. Sex-linked red is one of the newer colours and will no doubt progress from its current preliminary status to championship status in due course. The colour itself is a warm red, becoming a deeper shade at the hair tip. The undercoat is a red-apricot. The nose leather and paw pads are pink.

CREAM

This is the dilution of sex-linked red. It is a soft, warm cream that becomes deeper at the hair tips. The undercoat is cream, while the nose leather and paw pads are pink.

Before you visit a breeder to be completely won over by gorgeous Abyssinian kittens like these, be sure you are ready to commit to the responsibility of cat ownership.

Purchasing an
ABYSSINIAN CAT

Before the decision to purchase an Abyssinian is made, careful consideration should be given to the implications and responsibilities of cat ownership. If more owners would do this, there would be far fewer half-starved pets roaming our streets or having to live in local animal-rescue centres.

OWNER RESPONSIBILITY

The initial cost of an Abyssinian represents only a fraction of its lifetime's cost. The first question is, 'Can you afford one?' The kitten needs vaccinations to protect it against various diseases. Boosters are then required every year. Cat food is more costly than that for dogs. There is also the cost of cat litter every week. Periodic vet checks and treatment for illness or accident must be allowed for. When holidays are taken, you may need to board the pet at a cattery.

From the outset, there will be additional costs apart from that of the kitten. It will need a basket, carrying box, feeding and grooming utensils, scratching post, a few toys and maybe a collar. If

THE PURCHASING PROCESS

Never rush into the purchase of a companion that is to be given the freedom of your home and will become an integral part of your life. A pure-bred cat may live 20 or more years. This is a long time. It is very prudent to take all those steps that will minimise the chances of your ever regretting the choice you make. Once you have decided on the sex, age, reason for purchase (pet, show or breeding) and desired colour, proceed cautiously, heeding all of the advice given here. By following a planned process of selection, you will also gain much useful information.

DOCUMENTATION

When you take delivery of your kitten, certain paperwork should come with it:

1. Three- to five-generation pedigree.
2. Breeder-signed registration application form or change of owner registration form. This assumes the breeder has registered stock. If he has not, the kitten cannot be registered at a later date. It is worth less than the kitten with registration paperwork. You are not recommended to purchase a kitten from unregistered parents.
3. Certificates of health, vaccination and neutering, if this has been effected. Ideally, it is desirable that the kitten's parents have been tested negative for major diseases. Additionally, the breeder should know the blood group of your kitten. This may be of importance at a later date.
4. Details of worming or other treatments attended.
5. Diet sheet, feeding timetable and brand names of food items used. This diet should be maintained for at least ten days while the kitten adjusts to the trauma of moving home.
6. Signed receipt for monies paid.
7. Signed copy of any guarantees. Not all breeders give a guarantee on the reasonable grounds that once the kitten leaves their care, its onward well-being is no longer under their control.

you have any doubts at all about being able to supply all of these needs, it is best not to obtain a cat.

Other matters also need careful thought. If you are planning to have a family, will your love for the Abyssinian be compromised once a baby arrives? Cats generally are not a problem with family newcomers, providing they are not ignored or treated as being a threat to the baby. Never purchase a kitten for a child unless you want one yourself. If you are elderly, it is only fair to consider what would happen to your cherished pet if it were to outlive you or if you were to

become hospitalised for long periods.

It is most unfortunate that many people rush into the purchase of cats on impulse. They then find they cannot cope if problems, and extra costs, ensue. Some lose interest in the pet once it matures past its kitten stage. The evidence of these realities is easily seen in the growing number of cats abandoned or taken to animal shelters every year. Invariably their owners will make feeble excuses for why the cat cannot be kept, but the bottom line is they did not stop to consider at the outset what responsible ownership entailed.

The Abyssinian makes an ideal feline companion. Its conformation allows it to be full of mischief, and this tends to encourage interaction between cat and owner. This in turn creates a strong bond, which makes the breed a super companion. It has a soft voice and any potential owner would find little to fault in the behaviour patterns of this truly classic feline breed.

However, an Abyssinian not lovingly cared for throughout its life, and especially during its formative kitten weeks, can become a distrustful, shy and very aggressive cat—totally different from its genetic predisposition for its temperament.

The structure of an Abyssinian is crucial to its

Enchanting Aby kittens make it hard to resist taking the whole litter home with you, but use your head to make a carefully thought-out decision.

behaviour. The breed is very much the ideal build for a cat. It is powerful enough to easily haul its body up trees (or curtains) at a goodly pace; it is light enough to allow it to spring from one point to another with consummate ease (as from a shelf to your shoulder when playing games).

All cats are inquisitive by nature, but those with an athletic build have a greater ability to satisfy their curiosity than the heavily built breeds. They can easily spring onto cupboard tops, from where it is no problem to scale shelves or doors. This allows them to inspect ornaments and such (and maybe rearrange them or send them crashing to the floor). The beautifully natural build of the Aby means that it has an highly efficient metabolism that enables it to prolong its periods of activity for far longer than can heavier breeds.

The ability to satisfy its curiosity has an important side

TAKING KITTY HOME

Arrange collection of the kitten as early in the day as possible. If a long journey is involved, be sure to take a few breaks so that kitty does not suffer from travel sickness. Do not make stops to show the kitten to friends; this represents an health hazard. Once home, offer the kitten a drink, then allow it to sleep if it so requires. Children must be educated to handle a kitten gently, never to tease it and to respect its sleeping privacy. Until it is litter-trained, it should be restricted to the kitchen or another room with an easy-to-clean floor surface.

ENVIRONMENTAL INFLUENCES

It was often said in the past that the Aby tended to be a shy breed and did not like close confinement. This is not reflective of the breed's true character, but is more reflective of environmental conditions. The Aby has always been a connoisseur's breed, often kept by people living a quiet lifestyle. Any intrusion to an Aby's domain meant that it was apt to withdraw until it felt assured that visitors were friendly. Thus, the shyness was created by the type of owner and the cat's environment rather than being inherent to the breed.

Today more and more owners are keeping Abys (and all breeds) in relatively close confinement. It is normal for breeders and enthusiasts to say that the breed will thrive under such conditions. The reality is that the Aby has always been capable of adjusting to the lifestyle of its owners. However, like all cats, it enjoys the open air and will be less likely to become stressed if given access to this via aviary-like outdoor exercise pens, if confinement is needed.

effect not always appreciated when discussing traits such as intelligence and temperament. Nothing succeeds like success. Because the Aby can achieve so much as a consequence of its conformation, it will tend to constantly strive to find new things to do. Once accomplished at a given task, it will draw on this when it meets a similar situation. By this constant trial and error process, it will gain far more experiences than will the heavy breeds. It will appear to be more intelligent when in truth it is simply more experienced, or educated, depending on how you view this.

The short coat of the Abyssinian makes it a superior lap cat to the longhaired breeds, which quickly become too hot when reclining on a lap. However, the even less dense coat of the present-day Oriental breeds possibly makes them the ideal lap cats from this perspective. Suffice it to say, the Aby is a very good lap cat.

KITTEN OR ADULT?

Most potential owners normally want a kitten because it is so cute, cuddly and playful. A kitten is easily trained and has not yet developed bad habits, which the older Abyssinian may have done. This said, if you plan to breed or exhibit, there are advantages in obtaining a young adult. Other potential owners, such as the elderly, may benefit by avoiding the demanding needs of a young kitten. In both of these instances, a good age is when the youngster is 9–15 months old. Even a fully mature Abyssinian may prove an excellent choice for some owners.

Kittens should not be obtained under 12 weeks old, though 14–16 weeks is better. No reputable breeder will sell them younger than this. Less caring breeders will let them go to new homes as young as eight weeks of age. Such juveniles will barely have been weaned. They will not have developed the needed resistance to major diseases. They are more likely to become stressed by the premature removal from their mother and siblings. Their vaccinations will not be fully effective. These factors will dramatically increase the risk of immediate problems.

SEX & COLOUR PATTERN

If it is to be purely a pet, the Abyssinian's gender is unimportant. Both are delightful. Males are usually larger, bolder and more outgoing. Females tend to be more discerning about which humans they like. However, each Abyssinian is an individual. Its character and health, more than its sex, should be the basis of selection. Again, the sex is unimportant for the potential exhibitor. It is not even necessary

ADOPTING AN ADULT
Some owners, such as the elderly, may benefit by adopting an adult cat. They can avoid the demanding needs of a young kitten and enjoy the advantages of a well-trained adult, making grooming an easier task. Breeders and exhibitors also can benefit from purchasing an older cat because it is easier to assess the quality. Sometimes, though, older cats can have bad habits that are hard to break. So if you are thinking about obtaining an older cat, it is important to thoroughly investigate possible behavioural and health problems.

Visiting a litter of Aby kittens will be an exciting and somewhat overwhelming experience. Allow the breeder to guide you in your selection of the perfect Aby for you and your lifestyle.

for the cat to be sexually 'entire.' Classes for neuters are featured in shows.

Those with breeding aspirations are advised to obtain only females. All pet owners should regard neutering (males) and spaying (females) as obligatory. Today this can be effected at any age after eight weeks.

The colour pattern is a matter of personal preference. It should never be placed ahead of health and character. Some colours and patterns will be more readily available than others. The more popular varieties may be less costly than the rarer ones. This would generally not apply to prospective breeding or exhibition individuals, where type quality will be as important as colour or pattern.

LOOK BEFORE YOU LEAP
It is important that you meet as many Abyssinian breeders and kittens as you can. This gives you a good mental picture of what an healthy typical example should look like and cost for the quality and colour you want. Normally, you will get what you pay for. If you look for the cheapest kitten, there will be a sound reason why it is the cheapest!

The best place to start your search is a cat show. At large cat shows, most of the colour varieties will be on display. Purchase the show catalogue. It lists all of

the exhibitors and their addresses. You can see if any live in your immediate locality. Whenever possible, it is best to purchase locally so you can visit the home of the breeder. Some breeders will insist you do so in order to be satisfied that you will make a good owner.

Shows and breeders are advertised in the various cat magazines available from newsagents. You also can contact a major cat registry, which will supply a list of national and regional clubs, which are usually able to supply breeder lists. When visiting a breeder, always make an appointment. Try to visit no more than one a day. This reduces the risk that you may transport pathogens (disease-causing organisms) from one establishment to the next.

Selecting a good breeder is a case of noting the environment in which the cats are kept, the attitude of the owner to you and his cats and how friendly and healthy the kittens look. It is vital that the chosen kitty has an outgoing personality. It must not appear timid or very shy. This indicates a lack of breeder socialisation or a genetic weakness in its temperament. Either way, it is not a kitten you should select.

CHOOSING A KITTEN
If you choose the breeder wisely, and especially if a friend

Your local pet shop should have a variety of litter boxes and trays from which you may choose the type that best suits your needs.

AN HEALTHY KITTEN

Closely inspect any kitten before making a final decision. Keep in mind the following points:

Eyes and nose: Clean and clear with no signs of discharge.

Ears: Fresh-smelling and erect.

Coat: Healthy, not dull or dry.

Anal region: Clean with no staining of the fur.

Feet: Four toes on each foot, plus a dewclaw on the inside of each front leg.

Teeth: Correct bite.

There should be no signs of parasites or bald areas of fur. A potbelly may indicate worms.

recommends him, this will practically eliminate any problems related to your making a poor choice. However, a little knowledge on what to look for will not go amiss. Observe the kittens from a distance to ensure none is unduly lethargic, which is never a good sign. If any kitten displays signs of illness, this should bring to an end any further thoughts of purchase from that source. A reputable breeder would not allow a sickly kitten to remain within its litter.

It is always advisable to select a kitten that shows particular interest in you. Abyssinians are very discerning. If both of you are drawn to each other, this will greatly enhance the bonding essential for a strong relationship.

Once a particular kitten has been selected, it should be given a close physical inspection. The eyes and nose must show no signs of weeping or discharge. The ears will be erect and fresh-smelling. The coat should look healthy, never dry or dull. There must be no signs of parasites in the fur. There will be no bald areas of fur, nor bodily swellings or abrasions. Lift the tail and inspect the anal region. This must be clean, with no indication of congealed faecal matter. Any staining of the fur indicates current or recent diarrhoea.

The kitten must not display a potbelly. This may indicate

There are many kinds of scratching posts designed to keep your cat interested and occupied. Purchase a well-made post and it will provide many years of durable service.

worms or other internal disorders. Check the teeth to be sure of a correct bite. Bear in

mind that the jawbones do not develop at the same rate. Minor imperfections may correct themselves (they may also get worse), but major faults will not. Inspect the feet to see that there are four toes on each, plus a dewclaw on the inside of each front leg.

With respect to colour, there is no link between this and health. Any faults in the colour or its placement will only be of importance in breeding or exhibition individuals. The potential breeder/exhibitor should obtain a copy of the appropriate registry's official standard so that he is *au fait*

HOMEMADE TOYS

Cats love to play and pet shops have many cat toys to choose from. Sometimes, however, people give their cats homemade toys. These can be harmful to your cat, as they could have pieces that could break off and be swallowed. Only give your pet toys from the pet shop that have been proven safe for cats.

with all colour, pattern and bodily faults of the breed.

KITTY SHOPPING SPREE

Certain accessories should be regarded as obligatory and obtained before the kitten arrives at your home.

SCRATCHING POST

This will save the furniture from being abused while wearing the cat's nails down. There are many models, some being simple posts, while others are combined with play stations and sleeping quarters. These are the best for keeping a cat interested.

LITTER BOX(ES)

Some are open trays; others are domed to provide extra privacy. Some types have special bases in which odour removers are fitted.

CAT LITTER

There are numerous types on the market, each offering advantages and drawbacks. Avoid the low-cost types that contain a lot of dangerous dust. Use those that are fully biodegradable.

FOOD/WATER DISHES

Polished metal has the longest-wear life. Earthenware is less costly than metal and superior to the plastic types.

GROOMING TOOLS

These will comprise a good-quality bristle brush, a fine-toothed comb, nail trimmers and a soft chamois leather.

CAT COLLAR AND/OR HARNESS

Select elasticised collars. Be sure that a name and address disc or barrel is fitted to the collar. An harness must be a snug but comfortable fit for the cat.

CARRYING BOX

This is essential for transporting the cat to the vet or other places, as well as for home restriction when needed. Be sure that it is large enough to accommodate a fully-grown Abyssinian, not just a kitten. The choice is between collapsible models, soft plastic types and, the best choice, those made of wood or fibreglass.

Cat carriers are a necessity of cat ownership, though no cat welcomes the opportunity of being carted about in a crate. Nonetheless, the carrier is the only safe option for transport.

Double-bowl feeders are very convenient for feeding your cat. Go to your pet shop to purchase top-quality feeders, which should come in a variety of colours, styles and sizes.

There is nothing glamorous about purchasing a litter box, yet cat owners have few options in this regard. Consult your local pet shop to see a selection of boxes. Some cats do not accept a covered box, while others welcome the 'privacy.'

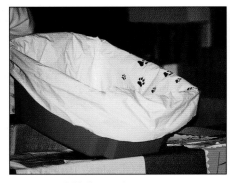

Liners are available for most litter trays to assist in keeping them clean and more manageable.

Purchasing a scratching post is a smart option for the cat owner. It's best to purchase a sturdy, well-made post that will last your cat years of utility.

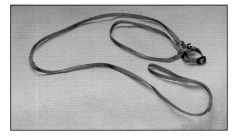

If you are considering walking your Abyssinian, you must have a lead that is suitable for a cat.

Providing a Safe Home for Your
ABYSSINIAN CAT

For a kitten, its human environment holds many dangers. Its owner must protect it from these hazards until it becomes agile and wiser. The following dangers lurk in typical households. Always check whether there are additional ones in your home. The most important decision you need to make from the outset is whether or not the kitten is to be given outdoor liberty.

HOW MUCH FREEDOM?

More than at any time in the past, the question of how much freedom a cat should be given is the subject of heated debate. It is a very subjective matter. Here the more pertinent points are given so you can relate these to your home location. This, to a very large degree, should influence your decision.

Cats living in or close to an urban area are at the highest safety risk. The amount of traffic is such that death from road accidents is a major concern. In such environments there are high dog populations, some of which are feral. Injury or death from dog attacks is therefore another major source of danger to a wandering feline.

Urban cat populations also are extremely high. Far too many cats are living a virtually feral existence. These are tough, street-wise cats that often carry fleas and other parasites that are vectors of disease. Some will be carriers of, or infected with, feline leukaemia and other deadly diseases.

The typical feline family pet can be badly injured if it becomes engaged in fights with these roaming bullies. Furthermore, their very presence in and around a gentle cat's garden can cause the pet severe stress. This can make it fearful of stepping outside its home. In some instances, it may cause the pet to actually leave its home.

Sadly, if these risks are not enough, there is no shortage of people who will steal a pedigreed cat, the more so if it is friendly. Add to this the number of abusive people who do not like cats roaming into their gardens, and the scenario is not good. Finally, free-roaming cats also take a heavy toll on local bird and wildlife populations.

Taking these various facts into account, the urban cat is best kept

THE TRAVELLING CAT

Whenever your cat needs to be taken on a car journey, never let it travel loose in the vehicle, which is illegal. It must always be in its carrying box. If a cat were to go under the clutch or brake pedal when the car was moving, this would be dangerous to all occupants. A cat might also spring from one seat to another, which might distract the driver. This could have disastrous results.

Never leave a cat alone in a car on an hot day. The temperature can rise dramatically to the point that the cat is unable to breathe. It could die of heat stroke. Always leave a window partially open when you are in the car with your cat, so that it can stay cool in its carrier.

enjoyment, even if this is restricted to the garden. When walking your cat in public places, use only an harness. This is much safer than a collar.

In contrast to urban situations, the cat living in a rural environment is far safer, the more so if there are no immediate neighbours or busy roads. Even so it is wise to restrict the cat's outdoor freedom to daylight hours. During the night, it is more likely to get run over or to threaten local wildlife.

Those living between the extremes of isolated areas and busy urban environments should consider the local risk factor. Generally, it is best to keep the cat indoors but to provide an outdoor exercise pen.

HOUSEHOLD DANGERS

Within its home, a kitten is best viewed as an accident waiting to happen! The most dangerous room is the kitchen. Hot electric hobs, naked flames from gas rings, boiling pans of food or water and sinks full of water are obvious hazards. An iron left on its board with cable trailing to the floor is an invitation to a kitten to jump up—with potentially fatal consequences. Washing machines or spin dryers with warm clothes in them, and their doors open, are inviting places to nap. Always check the kitty isn't inside if the door has been left open. Cup-

indoors. It can enjoy the benefit of the outdoors if supplied with a roomy aviary-type exercise pen. Some cats can be trained to walk on a lead. This allows outdoor

boards containing poisonous or other dangerous substances should always be kept securely closed.

In the living room, the normal dangers are aquariums without hoods, unguarded fires, electric bar heaters, poisonous indoor plants, trailing electrical leads, and ornaments that may be knocked over by a mischievous kitty. Toilets can be fatal to an over-curious kitten. The same is true of a bath containing water. Balconies should be safeguarded to remove the potential for the kitten to slip and fall.

OTHER DANGERS

Other potential dangers are when electric tools are left lying about and connected to power outlets— even worse if they are left on, as with bench saws. If the kitten is given freedom to exercise in a

BE ONE JUMP AHEAD
Seemingly innocuous things, such as doors, can become life-threatening should they suddenly slam shut on a kitten due to a strong draught. When windows and external doors are open, be sure internal doors are secured with a doorstop. At all times be one jump ahead of a kitten in terms of identifying dangerous situations.

DANGEROUS DISINFECTANTS
Although owners should disinfect the litter box regularly to prevent disease and illness, some household disinfectants can be harmful to cats. Pine-oil-based cleaners are toxic to cats. DO NOT use them. Products containing Phenol should also be avoided. Bleach is a good disinfectant to use; however, be sure to rinse the litter box thoroughly and air it out to get rid of any fumes.

garden containing a pond, the kitten must be under constant supervision. Cherished ornaments should be placed out of reach of the kitten, as much for their safety as to any danger they may present to the kitty. It's not always the direct danger of something that can be the problem. If an ornament or similar item crashes to the floor, this can startle the kitten into a panicked departure! The kitten could then fall from a shelf in its haste. It goes without saying that all safety measures discussed here are of equal importance for adult cats.

The breeder introduces young kittens to solid foods before they leave for their new homes. Your chosen breeder should provide you with a diet sheet to guide you in your selection of the best food for your Aby kitten.

ABYSSINIAN CAT

Today, the feeding of cats has been reduced to its most simple level with the availability of many scientifically prepared commercial diets. However, this fact can result in owners' becoming casual in their approach to the subject. While the main object of a given diet is to provide the ingredients that promote healthy growth and maximum immunity to disease, it also fulfils an important secondary role.

A proper diet must maintain in the cat a psychological feeling of well-being that avoids nutritionally related stress problems or syndromes. By ensuring that the diet is balanced, of good variety and never monotonous, these dual roles will be achieved. This approach also will avoid the situation of the cat's becoming a finicky eater.

BALANCE AND VARIETY

A balanced diet means one that contains all of the major ingredients—protein, fats, carbohydrates, vitamins and minerals—in the ratios needed to ensure maximum growth and health. Variety means supplying foods in a range of forms that will stimulate and

IMPORTANT DON'TS

- Do not let your cat become a fussy eater. Cats are not born fussy but are made that way by their owners. Your cat will not starve if given the correct food, but it may try to convince you otherwise. However, a cat that refuses all foods offered may be ill. If this happens, contact your vet.
- Do not give a cat sweet and sticky foods. These provide no benefit and, if eaten, will negatively affect normal appetite for wholesome foods.
- Do not feed vitamin and mineral supplements to either kittens or adults unless under advice from a veterinary surgeon. Excess vitamins and minerals can be as bad for your cat's health as a lack of them. They will create potentially dangerous cellular metabolic imbalances.
- Do not give any questionable foods, such as those that smell or look 'off.' If in doubt, discard them. Always store foods in cool, darkened cupboards. Be sure that all foods from the freezer and refrigerator are fully thawed.

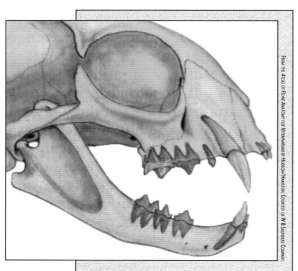

FROM THE ATLAS OF FELINE ANATOMY FOR VETERINARIANS BY HUDSON/HAMILTON. COURTESY OF W B SAUNDERS COMPANY.

MEET THE MEAT-EATERS

Since cats are carnivorous, their teeth are designed to bite and cut. Except for crunching dried foods, cats do very little chewing. They have the fewest teeth of any common domestic mammal—typically 30 (although there are some variations). The canine teeth usually are more developed than the incisors.

maintain the cat's interest in its meals. Commercially formulated foods come in three levels of moisture: low (dried foods), semi-moist and moist (tinned foods).

Generally, the dried and tinned foods are the most popular. Dried cat foods have the advantage that they can be left in the cat dish for longer periods of time than tinned foods. Dried foods are ideal for supplying on a free-choice basis. Like the tinned varieties, they come in a wide range of popular flavours.

In order to meet the specific needs of a kitten, there are specially formulated foods available. These contain higher protein levels needed by a growing kitten. As it grows, the kitten can be weaned slowly onto the adult types. There also are special brands available from vets for any kitten or cat that may have a dietary problem as well as special diets for the older cat. These may need lower ratios of certain ingredients, such as proteins and sodium, so as to reduce the workload of the liver.

Flavours should be rotated so that interest in meals is maintained. This also encourages familiarity with different tastes. Naturally, Abyssinians will display a greater liking for certain flavours and brands than for others.

FRESH FOODS

To add greater variety and interest, there are many fresh foods that Abyssinians enjoy. Some will be very helpful in cleaning the teeth and exercising the jaw muscles. All have the benefit of providing different textures and smells that help stimulate the palate. Feed these foods two or three times a week as treats or occasionally as complete meals.

Cooked poultry, including the skin but minus the bones, is usually a favourite, as is quality raw or cooked mincemeat. Cooked beef on the bone gives the cat something to enjoy. Cooked white fish, as well as tinned tuna or sardines, are examples of ocean delights. Never feed raw fish; this can prove dangerous, even fatal. Although cats rarely enjoy items such as rice, pasta or cooked vegetables, these can nonetheless be finely chopped and mixed with meats or fish. Some Abyssinians may develop a taste for them. Various cheeses and scrambled or boiled eggs will often be appreciated—but never give raw eggs.

If the diet is balanced and varied, the addition of vitamin and mineral supplements is unnecessary and can actually prove dangerous. While certain of these compounds are released from the body if in excess, others

ESTABLISHING DAILY INTAKE

Quoting amounts needed is impossible because of the varying factors mentioned. The best way to establish requirements is on an actual consumption basis. Place a small amount of food on the dish and see how quickly this is eaten. If all is devoured within a few minutes, add a little more. Repeat this until the kitten/cat is satiated and walks away from its dish. Do likewise at the other meals and you will quickly establish daily intake.

DIETARY DIFFERENCES BETWEEN CATS AND DOGS

You should never feed your cat dog food because dogs and cats have different dietary needs. Cats have a much higher need for fats than dogs, and kittens need more than adult cats. Cats also require unusually high levels of dietary protein as compared with those required by dogs. The foods you choose for your cat must supply these essential components.

are not. They are stored and can adversely affect efficient metabolism. If a cat shows loss of condition and disinterest in its food, discuss its diet with a vet.

HOW MUCH TO FEED

Food intake is influenced by many factors. These are the cat's age, activity level, the ambient temperature (more is eaten in the colder months), the cat's breeding

To guarantee that your Abyssinian maintains a magnificent shiny coat, only offer top-quality foods. The food you offer will have apparent effects on your cat's coat, behaviour and overall health.

state (rearing kittens) and the quality of the food. Always follow the breeder's recommendations on diet until your kitten has settled into your home. Thereafter, the needed quantity will increase as the kitten gets older, until full maturity at about two to three years of age.

As a basic guide, a four-month-old kitten will require four meals a day. At six months old, one meal can be dropped. By twelve months of age, only two meals will be required, possibly only one if dried foods are also available on a free-choice basis. As the number of meals is decreased, the quantity must be increased at the meals fed.

FOOD AND WATER CONTAINERS

Abyssinians are not too fussy over what vessels are used for supplying their food and water, but a few tips are useful. Abyssinians do not like to eat from dirty dishes any more than you would. Their food bowls should be washed after each meal. Water containers should be washed every day and replenished often. Saucers make ideal food plates. Wide feeders from your pet shop are excellent for dried biscuits. Pot or polished metal containers are better buys than plastic. They last longer and are easier to keep clean.

Like most cats, the Abyssinian

EAT YOUR HAIRBALLS AWAY
Food companies have developed formulas containing a wholesome fibre blend that moves ingested hair through the cat's digestive tract, thus minimising the occurrence of hairballs. Tests show that feeding these formulas moved 80% more hair through the digestive tract, resulting in fewer hairballs!

does not like to place its head into deep food dishes nor do they like their whiskers to touch the inner walls. Ensure that dishes are wide and shallow.

WHERE AND WHEN TO FEED

Usually, the best place to feed a cat is in the kitchen. It is important to place food and water dishes as far away from the litter tray as possible; feeding near the litter tray could deter the cat from eating. Cats also like to eat in quiet comfort. Meals should be spread across the entire day. When the number is reduced to two, these should be given in the morning and evening at convenient times. For the Abyssinian given outdoor freedom, it is best to feed the main meal in the evening. This encourages the cat to come home at this time. It can then be kept indoors overnight.

Grooming Your
ABYSSINIAN CAT

From the perspective of grooming, the Abyssinian has an easy non-matting coat. If brushed every day, it will rarely need combing, though this is beneficial. Brisk brushing followed by a polish, using a chamois leather or piece of silk cloth, will maintain the fur in super condition. If you frequently stroke your Abyssinian, the natural oils on your hand will give the coat a sleek look.

Regular grooming also enables close examination of the cat for any signs of problems. These include fleas or mites, small wounds, abrasions, swellings and bald areas. The grooming process should include inspection of the cat's ears, teeth and nails.

BRUSHING
Place the cat on a table of an height enabling you to comfortably control and groom the kitty. It can be useful to place white paper on the table. If any fleas are present, you will more easily notice them if they are groomed out of the fur. If the grooming is carried out gently, cats enjoy the experience. You should start when your Abyssinian is still a kitten.

Commence by brushing the fur on the back of the neck. Work along the back and down the sides, then down the legs and

HAIRBALLS (Trichobezoar)
When cats self-groom, they invariably swallow some of their hairs. Normally, these do not create a problem. However, if many dead hairs are in the coat, these may be licked and swallowed to accumulate in the stomach as hairballs. These are more common in longhaired breeds than in those with short hair. Hairballs may create intestinal blockages that may so irritate the cat's intestinal tract that it vomits the hairball or voids it via its faecal matter.

If the hairball is not removed, and the cat displays reduced appetite, veterinary assistance is needed. Regular grooming greatly reduces the risk of this condition. Additionally, a teaspoon of liquid paraffin or another laxative once a week may be helpful in cats prone to this problem. A laxative, however, is unlikely to remove an existing hairball. Pineapple juice containing the enzyme bromelain may break down small furballs. One teaspoonful a day for three days is the recommended dosage.

finally the tail. The abdominal area must be brushed more gently, as it is very sensitive.

Next, repeat the process using the fine-toothed comb, then comb against the lie of the hair. This will enable you to see if there are any parasites present. These often favour the tail base or the neck, behind the ears. Next, comb with the lie of the fur. Add a final lustre by brushing with the chamois.

BATHING
Occasionally, even shorthaired cats may need bathing. This may be of the wet or dry type. For wet

GROOMING EQUIPMENT
For total grooming needs, the following are required:
1. Semi-stiff bristle brush or rubber-pinned brush
2. Fine-toothed comb
3. Flea comb
4. Thin chamois leather and/or a silken cloth
5. Pair of guillotine-type nail trimmers
6. Medium-soft toothbrush
7. Cat toothpaste
8. Supply of cotton wool and cotton buds
9. Bottle of baby oil

Start combing and brushing your Aby when it is still young. This will accustom your kitten to the grooming process so that it will accept grooming as an adult.

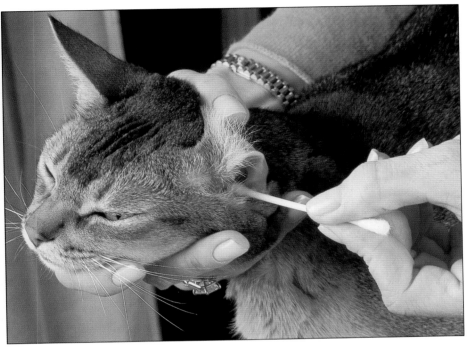

Never probe into your Aby's ear canal with a cotton bud. Only the outer part of the ear should be cleaned, using a careful and gentle touch.

baths, using the kitchen sink is preferable to a bath. This saves bending and allows for better

DRY SHAMPOO

A dry bath may be preferred to a wet one during very cold weather or when the cat is not well enough for a water bath. Sprinkle dry shampoo onto the coat and give it a good brushing. This will remove excess grease and dirt without being as thorough as a wet bath. Be very sure that all of the powder is brushed from the fur to avoid potential irritation and consequential scratching.

control of the cat. To prevent the cat from sliding, use a rubber mat. A spray attachment is more efficient than a jug to wet and rinse the coat. The cat should have its own towels.

The choice of shampoo is important. It ideally should be formulated for cats—do not use one for dogs. This could cause problems on a cat's coat. Baby shampoos are the best alternative. Dry shampoos in powder form are available from pet shops. Alternatives would be talcum powder, powdered chalk or heated bran flakes.

The kitten should be bathed

> **HAIR, HAIR EVERYWHERE!**
> Cat's hairs grow denser on the abdomen than on the back. The hairs grow according to both light periodicity (daylight versus dark nights) and temperature. Outdoor cats living in colder climates cast their coats twice a year, in the spring and fall, while house cats do so all year long.

by the time it is six months of age. This will familiarise it with the process before it matures and the process degenerates into a pitched battle. Cats have no love of bathing but can come to accept it if it does not become an unpleasant ordeal.

Grooming should always precede bathing, as this will remove any dead hairs. The key to success lies in ensuring that no water or shampoo is allowed to enter and irritate the eyes or ears. You should be able to cope single-handed with a kitten. However, it may be prudent to have someone else present just in case the adult proves more of a super cat than a kitten!

The water temperature should be warm, never cold or too hot. Prepare a shampoo and water solution before commencing. Have a large towel at hand. Commence by soaking the fur of the neck, then work along the back, sides, legs and tail. Pour shampoo onto the back and work this in all directions until the cat has been fully shampooed. Next, thoroughly rinse all shampoo away. It is essential that none be left, otherwise, it may cause later irritation. Gently but firmly squeeze all water from the coat. The face can be cleaned using a dampened flannel.

Wrap the kitten in the towel and give it a brisk rubbing until it is as dry as possible. It can then be allowed to dry naturally, after which it can be given a final brush and polish. If the cat is normally allowed outdoors, do not allow this for some hours until you are sure the coat is dry. In the colder months, it is best to attend to bathing in the early evening and keep the cat indoors overnight. The use of an hand dryer is not essential on a short-coated breed, but does shorten the drying time.

EARS, EYES AND NAILS

When inspecting the ears, look for any signs of dirt. This can be

> **HAIR GROWTH**
> Cat's body hairs grow from the follicles, which are connected to the dermis. Tactile hairs (whiskers) are thicker and longer, originating three times deeper than the normal body hairs.

PRESS-ON NAILS!

A stylish and fairly successful inhibitor of scratching is a plastic covering on the nails. A plastic sheath is placed over each nail and glued on with a strong, permanent adhesive. Depending upon the cat's activity, these sheaths last from one to three months.

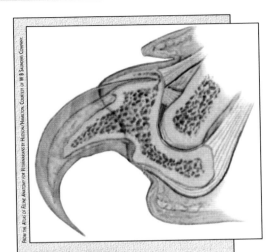

gently wiped away using a dampened cotton bud or one with just a little baby or vegetable oil on it. Never attempt to probe into the ear. If the ear is very waxed, this may indicate any of various health problems. A visit to the vet is recommended. The corner of the eyes can be gently wiped with damp cotton wool to remove any dust that occasionally accumulates.

Inspection of a cat's claws is achieved by firstly restraining it while on its back on your lap or held against your chest. Hold the paw and apply pressure to the top of this with your thumb. The nail will appear from its sheath. If the nail needs trimming, use the appropriate trimmers.

It is vital that you do not cut into, or even too close to, the quick, which is a blood vessel. This can be seen as a darker area of the nail in pink-clawed cats. It is more difficult, or not possible, to see the quick in dark-coloured nails. In such instances, trim less.

DECLAWING

Declawing is the surgical removal of all of the claw (or nail) and the first toe joint. This practice is heavily frowned upon and even illegal in some countries, such as the United Kingdom. Unfortunately, in some areas of the world, this procedure is still performed. Some owners only have the claws from the front feet removed; others do all four feet. An alternative surgical procedure is one that removes the tendon that allows the cat to protract its claws. This procedure, referred to as a tendonectomy, as compared to an onychectomy (removal of the claws), is less traumatic for the cat. Claws still must be filed and trimmed after a tendonectomy.

Declawing is not always 100% successful. In two-thirds of the cases, the cats recovered in 72 hours. Only 4–5% of the cats hadn't recovered within a fortnight. About 3% of the cats had their claws grow back!

Abys, like most other cats, rarely enjoy having their nails clipped. If your cat isn't wearing down his nails naturally, you will have to clip them to dissuade your cat from clawing your furniture and belongings.

You may need an helper to do the trimming or the holding. If in doubt, let your vet do this for you. If cats have ample access to scratching posts, they will only infrequently, if ever, require their nails to be trimmed.

TEETH

From its youngest days, your kitten should become familiar with having its teeth cleaned. Many owners do not give teeth the attention they should. This has become progressively more important due to the soft-diet regimens of modern cats. Initially,

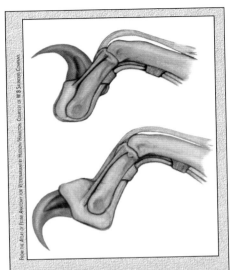

RETRACTABLE CLAWS

When at rest, a cat's claws are retracted. The muscles hold the claws in their sheaths. The claw is then extended if the cat wishes to attack prey, defend itself, grab an object or climb. That is why your cat's claws are not always visible. This is true for all species of felines except the cheetah, which is unable to retract its claws, except when it is very young.

Cleaning the eyes with a soft cotton wipe will keep them free of debris and dust. This should become a regular part of your grooming process.

gently rub the kitten's teeth, using a soft cloth on which toothpaste has been placed. This will accustom the kitten to having its teeth touched as well as to the taste of the tooth cleaner. When this is no problem for the kitten, you can progress to a soft toothbrush and ultimately one of medium hardness. Periodically let your vet check the cat's mouth.

Abys are intelli-
gent and
attentive
students, capable
of being trained
as effectively as
most other
members of the
feline clan.

ABYSSINIAN CAT

One of the outstanding virtues of cats is that they are easy to live with. They are fastidious in their personal habits related to grooming and toilet routines and basically require very little of their owners. Nonetheless, behavioural problems in cats can occur, and an owner needs to understand all of the possible causes and solutions. You may never encounter a single problem with your cat, but it pays to be prepared should your feline charge disrupt your domestic bliss.

THE BASIS OF TRAINING

The most effective means of training a cat is via reinforcement of success. A cat learning from lavish praise of doing what is required will want to repeat the action to gain more affection. There are no potential negative side effects. Conversely, when scolding or another method of discipline is used, there is always the possibility that the cat will not relate the punishment to what the owner had intended.

For example, you cannot discipline for something done in the past. The past is anything much longer than a few minutes

SETTING THE GROUND RULES

From the outset, you must determine the ground rules and stick to them. Always remember that your companion's patterns of behaviour begin to form from the moment it first arrives at your home. If the future adult is not to be given outdoor freedom, then do not let it outdoors as a kitten. If any rooms are to be out of bounds to the adult, then do not let the kitten into them. Stability is vital in a cat's life; without it, the result will be stress and its related behavioural changes.

Ground rules of how to handle the kitten and to respect its privacy when sleeping should be instilled into all children. The cat's meals should be given at about the same time each day. This will have the secondary advantage that the pet's toilet habits will be more predictable.

MAN MEETS CAT

Early man, perhaps 8000 years ago, started his symbiotic relationship with domestic cats, *Felis catus* or *Felis domesticus*. The cats killed and ate the rats and mice and probably anything else that crawled and was small, which early man attracted and considered as pests. Early man reciprocated by allowing the cat to sleep in his cave, hut or tent. Cats, being essentially nocturnal, kept the small mammals (rats, mice, etc.) from disturbing the sleep of early man.

As early man evolved to modern man, the domestic cat came along as an aid to pest control. This was especially true of peoples who farmed, as farmers were plagued with rodents. Though most cats were not selectively bred for their predatory skills, it was obvious that those cats that were the best hunters were more successful in evolutionary terms than the cats that were more meek. Modern cats have changed very little from the cats from which they descended. There are still, today, cats that are very predatory, attacking small mammals and birds; there are also meek cats which, unless fed by their owners, would perish in a competitive cat society.

It has been shown repeatedly that if kittens are socialised in a proper manner, they will become peaceful pets. If the kittens are not socialised properly, they revert immediately to their aggressive, predatory behaviours.

ago. If you call the cat to you and punish it for something done hours earlier, it cannot relate to that action. It will relate the discipline to the act of going to you when called! This will create insecurity in the pet, increasing the risk that more problems will develop.

REMEDIAL METHODS

When faced with a problem, firstly try to pinpoint the likely cause(s). Next, consider the remedial options. Be sure that these remedies will not result in negative side effects linked to you. Always be the paragon of patience. Some problems may be extremely complex and deeply rooted within the cat's behaviour patterns. As such, they are habits not easily changed and often difficult to analyse. In discussing the following problems, it is hoped that you will understand the basic ways to correct other unwanted patterns of behaviour that might occur. But always remember, it is far better to avoid a problem than to correct it.

THE LITTER TRAY

A very common problem for some owners is that their cat starts to attend to its toiletry needs anywhere other than in its litter tray. The problem may become apparent from the time the kitten gets to its new home, or it may

CATS AND OTHER PETS

If you already have a pet cat or dog, or almost any animal that isn't small, creeping or crawling, your cat can usually be socialised so the other pet and the cat will tolerate each other. In many cases, cats and dogs become quite friendly and attached to each other, often making frequent physical contacts, sleeping together or even sharing each other's toys.

develop at any time during its life. So, let us start from the beginning and try to avoid the situation.

Until you are satisfied that the kitten is using its litter tray, do not give it access to carpeted rooms. The youngster should already have been litter-trained

THE TRUTH ABOUT CATS AND DOGS

Cats are unique in having the scrotum fully haired, a marked difference from their canine counterparts. This led one early observer to say that cats were not small dogs! Dogs were domesticated well before cats since cats only served to protect the abode of the owner from rodents, while dogs served as guards, hunters, herders, exterminators and loyal companions that were readily trainable. Cats have always been more independent and less trainable.

well before you obtained it. You should buy a litter tray similar to the one it is already familiar with. It is also important that the same brand of litter is used, at least initially. Place the tray in a quiet spot so the kitten has privacy when attending to its needs.

A kitten will need to relieve itself shortly after it has eaten, exercised or been sleeping. Watch

it carefully at these times. If it stoops to attend to its needs other than in the litter tray, calmly lift it into its tray and scratch at the litter. Never shout or panic the kitty by making a sudden rush for it. If it does what is hoped, give it lots of praise. If it steps out of the tray, gently place it back in for a few seconds.

If nothing happens, be patient and wait, then repeat the process. If it fouls the kitchen floor when you are not watching, simply

Monitor your Aby's activities carefully before you attempt to modify inappropriate behaviour. Climbing, jumping and scratching are normal everyday activities that you will never be able to stop entirely.

Using a litter box comes naturally to most kittens, who immediately accept the box for their toileting needs.

clean this up and wait for the next opportunity to transport the kitten to its tray. It rarely takes long for a kitten to consistently use the litter tray. Be very sure the tray is kept spotless. Cats have no more desire to use a fouled toilet than you do. Every few days, give the cat tray a good wash using soapy water and always rinse it thoroughly. Allow it to dry, then fill the tray with litter to depth of about 4–5 cms (1.5–2 inches).

By identifying the cause(s) of litter-box problems, the correction is often self-evident. However, once the cause has been corrected this is only part of the solution. Next, the habit of fouling other places must be overcome. Where possible, do not let the cat enter rooms it has started to foul until the odour has had time to fully disperse. Wash the area of the fouling, then treat carpets and soft furnishings with an odour neutraliser (not an air freshener) from your pet shop or vet.

If the cat cannot be prevented from entering certain rooms, then cover previously fouled areas with plastic sheeting or tinfoil, or rinse the fouled area with white vinegar (which cats hate!). Also, place a litter tray in the fouled room while the retraining is underway. It may help if a different size, type or colour of tray is used.

SCENT MARKING

Both sexes scent mark, though males are more prolific. It is a means of advertising their presence in a territory, thus an integral part of their natural

TIDY TOILETING

During the kitten's stay in the nest box, the mother will assist or even stimulate bowel and urine elimination, at least for the first month of the kitten's life. The mother also does the clean-up work in the nest box. Once the kitten is older, it becomes capable of relieving itself out of the nest box. Usually the kitten likes sand, soft earth or something that seems absorbent and is easily moved with its paws. By the time the kitten is two months old, it should develop the discipline of covering its elimination. Not all kittens develop this discipline, though the use of an absorbent clay litter seems to be helpful in developing this discipline in young cats. Your local pet shop will have various cat litters to offer you.

CAUSES OF LITTER-BOX PROBLEMS

1. The litter tray is dirty. Cats never like to use a previously fouled tray.
2. The litter has been changed to one of a different texture that the cat does not like. Generally the finer-grained litters are the most favoured.
3. A scented litter is being used to mask odours. The cat may not like the scent. Such litters should not be necessary if the tray is regularly cleaned.
4. The tray is regularly cleaned, but an ammonium or pine-based disinfectant is being used. This may aggravate the cat's sensitive nasal mucous membranes. Additionally, the phenols in pine are dangerous to cats.
5. The litter tray is located too close to the cat's food and water bowls. Cats do not like to eat near litter trays or to defecate/urinate close to their feeding areas.
6. Another cat or free-roaming pet has been added to the household and is causing the cat stress. In multi-cat households, two or more trays may be needed.
7. There is insufficient litter in the tray. There should be about 5 cms (2 inches) of litter depth.
8. The cat has developed a fear of using the tray due to an upsetting experience. For instance, the owner may have caught the cat as it finished using the tray in order that it could be given a medicine. Children may be disturbing it while it is relieving itself.
9. The cat is ill (or elderly) and is unable to control its bowel movements. Veterinary attention is required.
10. The cat, because of one or more of the previous problems, has established other more favourable areas.

behaviour. Spraying usually is done against a vertical surface. It tells other males that the individual is residing in that territory. Alternatively, it will tell a female that a male lives close by—or it will tell the male that a female is in the area. It is thus a very important part of a cat's social language.

Neutered cats have little need to mark their territory or leave their 'calling card' to attract mates. They are far less likely to spray than those not altered.

However, scent marking may commence when the cat is attempting to assert its position in the household.

To overcome the problem of scent marking, you first need to try and identify if there is an obvious specific cause. In multi-cat households, it also requires positive identification of the sprayer(s) and the favoured spraying surface. Giving the cat more freedom may help, and its own sleeping place if it does not have one. Covering the sprayed

Do not allow your cat to roam in your carport where it can encounter dangerous items such as toxic paints and chemicals.

surface with plastic sheeting or a cloth impregnated with a scent the cat does not like (such as lemon, pepper or bleach) may be successful. Spraying the cat with a water pistol when catching it in the action is a common ploy. Veterinary treatment with the hormone progesterone may prove effective—discuss this with your vet.

SCRATCHING
Scratching is a normal feline characteristic. Unfortunately, house cats tend to destroy the furniture to satisfy their need to scratch. Feral or outdoor cats usually attack a tree because trees are readily accessible and the bark of the tree suits their needs perfectly. If the outdoor cat lives in a pride, it will scratch more than a solitary feral cat. The

reasons for this are known. When cats scratch, they leave telltale marks. Parts of the nails' sheaths exudate from glands located between their claws, and the visual aspects are the marks that cats leave to impress or advertise their presence.

Cat owners whose cats scratch should not consider the scratching as an aggressive behavioural disorder. It is normal for cats to scratch. Keeping your cat's claws clipped or filed so they are as short as possible without causing bleeding may inhibit scratching. Your vet can teach you how to do this. Clipping and filing should be started when the kitten is very young. Starting this when the cat has matured is much more difficult and may even be dangerous.

There are ways to control

WHY WHISKERS?

Cats are famous for their whiskers. The whiskers are tactile hairs by which cats feel. Most tactile hairs are on the cat's face, mostly on the upper lip and around the eyes, and on the wrist (carpus). The carpal hairs are extremely sensitive and are found on many predatory animals that use their front paws for holding their victims.

annoying cat scratching. Certainly, the easiest way is to present your cat with an acceptable cat scratching post. These usually are available at most local pet shops. The post should be covered with a material that is to your cat's liking. If your cat has already indicated what it likes to scratch, it usually is a good idea to cover the post with this same material. Veterinary surgeons often suggest that you use sandpaper, as this will reduce the cat's nails quickly

and it will not have the urge to scratch. Certainly using hemp, carpeting, cotton towelling or bark is worth a try. Once the cat uses the post, it usually will have neither a desire nor a need to scratch anyplace else.

Besides the physical need to scratch, cats have a psychological need to scratch. This is evidenced by where they scratch versus what they scratch. Often cats prefer semi-darkness. Some prefer flat surfaces and not vertical surfaces. Some prefer public areas in which

FERAL CATS

Feral cats, as a general rule, are under-nourished. They spend most of their time searching for food. Consequently, those feral cats that have kittens spend less time with their kittens than do well-nourished cats. It has been shown that kittens born to feral mothers are usually unsocial and show little affection for their mothers. Obviously, they would show a similar lack of affection for a human. That's one of the reasons that feral kittens make poor pets and should neither be adopted nor taken into your home. Kittens that for any reason are separated from their mothers at the age of two weeks develop an attitude of fear and wariness. They escape from contact with other cats and humans and can even be dangerous if they feel trapped.

their human friends are present instead of secluded areas. It may be stress-related, as with scent marking, because scratching is another territory-marking behaviour. In any case, the idea is to get your cat to scratch the post and not the carpets, furniture, drapes or duvet on your bed.

Introduce your cat to the post by rubbing its paws on the post, hoping it will take the hint. Oftentimes the cat voluntarily attacks the post. Unfortunately, oftentimes it doesn't. If you catch your cat scratching in a forbidden area, startle it with a loud shout, banging a folded newspaper against your hand or something else that will take its attention away from scratching. Never hit

Kittens that are introduced to scratching posts at a young age will accept the devices readily and use them throughout their lives.

CAUSES OF SCENT MARKING

1. Another cat, or pet, has been introduced to the household. It may be bullying the resident cat. This problem may resolve itself when the two get to know each other. The more cats there are, the longer it may take for the situation to be resolved. Much will depend on the space within which the cats may roam and whether they are able to avoid those they dislike.
2. The birth of a new family member may annoy the cat for a while, especially if its owner suddenly gives it less attention.
3. A friend staying in the home for a few days may not like cats. If 'shooed' away a number of times, the cat may feel it should assert its position and mark it.
4. If the cat is given outdoor freedom, a bully may have moved into the territory. Having lost control of its own garden, the pet may assert its territorial boundaries within its home. If a cat flap is used, another cat may be entering the home and this will trigger the resident to scent mark.

the cat. This will only get a revengeful reaction that might be dangerous.

RUBBISH RUMMAGING
Cats are inquisitive and may decide to have a good look through any interesting rubbish

bins that are exuding enticing odours. Normally, the answer is to remove the bin. However, if the attraction always seems to be to the kitchen rubbish, there may be a nutritional problem. The cat may be searching for food because it is being underfed! It alternatively may be receiving an unbalanced diet and is trying to satisfy its inner need for a given missing ingredient.

Another possibility, and one that may be more appropriate to the indoors-only cat, is boredom and/or loneliness. These conditions only can be remedied by greater interaction between owner and cat and/or obtaining a companion feline.

Clearly, the cause should be identified. The immediate solution is to place the rubbish in a cupboard or similar place that is out of the cat's reach. This type of solution is called removal of the re-enforcer. It is a common method of overcoming problems across a number of unwanted behaviours. However, it does not correct the underlying problem, which must still be addressed.

The first-time cat owner should not think that the problems discussed will likely be encountered. They are only met when the cat's environment is lacking in some way. Always remember that the older cat may have problems with bowel control. An extra litter tray at another location in the home usually will remedy this situation. Finally, if a problem is found and you are not able to remedy it, do seek the advice of your vet or breeder.

SCRATCHING FURNITURE

All cats need to scratch in order to maintain their claws in good condition. For this reason, one or more scratching posts strategically placed in the cat's most-used rooms will normally prevent the problem. Place the post in front of the scratched furniture. It can be moved steadily further away once the furniture is ignored. This is a problem that may become more manifest when cats are not allowed outdoors and have insufficient indoor provisions to scratch.

Breeding Your

ABYSSINIAN CAT

CAVEAT EMPTOR

When purchasing a kitten for breeding, make certain that the seller knows what your intentions are. If a kitten is registered on the non-active register, this means it was not considered by its breeder to be good enough for breeding. Any kittens bred from such a cat cannot be registered. You should also check that the mother of the kitten/young adult in which you are interested has tested negative for FeLV, FIP and FIV and that all vaccinations are current.

While the idea of becoming a breeder may appeal to many owners, the reality is more difficult than often is appreciated. It requires dedication, considerable investment of time and money and the ability to cope with many heart-wrenching decisions and failures.

It would be quite impossible to discuss the complexities of practical breeding in only one chapter, so we will consider the important requirements of being a breeder plus basic feline reproductive information. This will enable you to better determine if, indeed, this aspect of the hobby is for you.

BEING A BREEDER

Apart from great affection for the breed, a successful breeding programme requires quantifiable objectives. Foremost among these is the rearing of healthy kittens free from known diseases. Next is the desire to produce offspring that are as good as, indeed better than, their parents.

Such objectives ensure that a breeder will endeavour to maintain standards and reduce or remove from the breed population any instances of dangerous diseases and conditions. Only stock registered and tested free of major diseases should ever be used. Adopting such a policy helps to counteract those who breed from inferior and often unhealthy cats.

To be a successful breeder, you will need to become involved

Responsible breeders produce kittens for both exhibition and companionship, always keeping the best interest of the breed first in their minds.

in the show competition side of the hobby. Only via this route will you be able to determine if your programme is successful or not. Always remember that even the top-winning breeders still produce quite an high percentage of kittens that will only be of pet quality. There will be many disappointments along the road to even modest success.

THE DISADVANTAGES OF BREEDING

There are many rewards to be gained from breeding, but the disadvantages also should be considered carefully. Kittens are demanding, especially once they are over three weeks of age. Rearing, vaccination, registration and veterinary bills will be costly. Any thoughts of profit should be dispelled. Homes must be found for the kittens, which will entail receiving many telephone calls—some at very inconvenient hours.

Many potential buyers will prove to be either unsuitable or 'time wasters' looking for the cheapest pedigreed cat obtainable. Kittens may die, while cats of any

TOO MANY CATS

There are already too many cats in the world. In many countries, thousands of pathetic-looking felines can be seen wandering the streets in a badly emaciated state. They lead tormented lives and have become a major social problem in many areas. There can be no excuse for these feral populations in developed Western nations. Quite frankly, some people who own cats, including some pedigreed owners, lack a sense of responsibility.

Cats allowed to roam in a non-neutered state are by far the main reason for the overpopulation problem. Unless a cat is of show or breeding quality, there is not a single justification for it to be bred or to remain in a non-neutered state. If your cat was purchased as a pet, you should help to resolve this global problem by having it neutered at the earliest possible date. This will make it a far healthier, happier and less problematic pet.

TOM FOOLERY

A non-neutered male cat kept as a single pet has little or no value for breeding purposes. It must be exhibited so it can gain some fame. The owner must have modern facilities to house both males and females. Females are always serviced at the home of the stud owner. This is extra responsibility and cost.

Such a male cannot be given any freedom to roam. If the tom is kept indoors, its scent-marking odours will often become intolerable. Even kept outdoors in a suitable cat pen, it will spray regularly to attract the attention of any females in the area. Toms are more assertive and often

more aggressive than neutered males. If they are allowed any outdoor freedom, they will become involved in battles with the local toms. Consequently, they will soon lose their handsome looks!

Most cat breeders do not even keep males because of the problems and costs they entail. These cats are best kept in catteries where the owners have the time, the funds and everything else needed to justify their retention.

age could test positive for a major disease. They may have to be put to sleep or given to a caring person who understands the problem.

Owning a number of cats will mean investing in cat pens. When females come into heat, they may try to escape and mate with any local tom with a twinkle in his eye! Their scent and calls will attract roving Romeos who will gather near your home and involve themselves in a series of raucous battles. Holidays and matings will need to be planned around hoped-for litter dates. All in all, owning only one or two breeding females is a major commitment.

Before deciding whether breeding really is something you want to do, what would make good sense would be to neuter the pet and then become an exhibitor. When you have exhibited a number of times, your knowledge of cats will be greater, as will your contacts. You will be more aware

ROAMING ROMEOS

Males cats, toms, have extended testicles very early in life. By about nine months of age, the tom is capable of mating with a queen. Both queens and toms are polygamous and it is not uncommon for a queen to have a litter containing kittens fathered by different toms.

CAT CALLS

Females left in a non-spayed state are far more at risk from diseases and infections of the uterus. When in heat, the female becomes unusually affectionate and provocative. Her calls, a sound once heard never forgotten, can become extremely annoying if she is left unmated.

WHAT'S A PEDIGREE WORTH?

When choosing breeding stock, never be dazzled by a pedigree. No matter how illustrious this is, it is only ever as good as the cat that bears it. If the cat is mediocre, then its prestigious pedigree is worthless from a breeding perspective. There are many other pitfalls for the novice when judging the value of a breeding line. These you must research in larger, more specialised books.

of what quality is all about, and what it will cost for a well-bred female. It will be like an apprenticeship. Whether you then become a breeder, remain an exhibitor or prefer life as a pet owner, you will be glad you heeded the words of advice given here.

STOCK SELECTION

Stock selection revolves around health, quality, sex and age. Before these are discussed, it should be stated that many beginners unwisely rush this process. It is essential that ample time be devoted to researching from whom to purchase. This decision will influence a novice breeder's future endeavours.

HEALTH

Cats only should be obtained from a breeder whose stock has been tested negative for the cat diseases known as FeLV, FIP and FIV. The stock should be current on all vaccinations and worm treatments. Additionally, its blood type should be known so as to avoid incompatibility problems.

QUALITY

This must come in two forms. One is in the individual cat's appearance; the other is in its genetic ability to pass on the quality of its parents. The best way of obtaining these paired needs is to obtain initial stock

THE BREEDING QUEEN

A female used for breeding purposes is called a queen. The principal requirement of such a cat is that she is an excellent example of the breed. This does not mean necessarily that she must be a show winner. Many a winning exhibition cat has proved to have little breeding value. This is because a show cat gains success purely on its appearance; however, it may not pass on those looks to its offspring.

A good breeding female may lack that extra something needed to be a top winner. Yet, she may pass on most of her excellent features to her offspring. Much will depend on the breeding line from which she was produced. Therefore, any potential breeder must research existing breeders to ascertain which have good track records of producing consistently high-quality cats. In truth, and sadly, few newcomers in their haste to become breeders make this extra effort. This can result in becoming disillusioned if the female produces only average to inferior kittens.

from a breeder having a proven record of success with Abyssinians, and with the colour you plan to start with. Being well acquainted with the breed's standard will be advantageous when seeking foundation stock. A female show cat attains her titles based on her appearance, but she may not pass on those looks to her offspring. Another cat that is very sound may pass on most of her good points and thus be more valuable for breeding. Of course, all litters will be influenced by the quality of the tom used. He will account for 50% of the offspring's genes. When viewing a litter of kittens, never forget that they are the result of the genes of two cats.

SEX

The beginner should obtain only females. The best advice is to commence with just one very sound female. By the time you have exhibited her and gained more knowledge about the finer points of the breed, you will be better able to judge what true quality is all about. By then, you also will have made many contacts on the show circuit. Alternatively, you may decide that breeding is not for you and will have invested the minimum of time and money. A male is not needed until a breeder has become established. Even then, owning one is not essential to success. There is no shortage of

Producing a trio of splendid Aby kittens such as this requires years of commitment and experience. Success in cat breeding relies upon the breeder's dedication and responsibility.

in shows. This will be when she is 14 weeks to 9 months of age, but she will be more costly.

3. A quality young female that has already produced offspring is a prudent choice but will be the most expensive option.

THE MALE STUD

The selection of a suitable stud should have been planned months before, as it can take some time to find the best male to use. It is preferred that the breeding lines of the stud are compatible with those of the female, meaning that both pedigrees will carry a number of the same individuals in them. This is termed line-breeding. The ideal male will excel in those features that are considered weak in the female. You may read in other books that if a female is weak in a given feature, the ideal stud will be the total opposite. However, this can be misleading.

If the female has an overly long tail, what you do not need is a stud with a short tail. Rather, his tail should be as near the ideal length as possible. Genetically, this will improve tail length in your line without introducing unwanted genetic variance in your stock. Compensatory matings, such as short tail to long tail, will create such a variance. Once a male has been selected, ensure that all of his papers and vaccinations are in order. The female will be taken to the stud and left with him for a few days.

Most breeders begin with a female, as the male is much too difficult to keep in a whole (non-neutered) state. quality studs. Males create many problems that the novice can do without. Once experience is gained is the time to decide if owning a male would be of any particular benefit.

AGE

There is no specific age at which stock should be purchased, but the following are suggested:

1. Most people purchase young kittens so they can enjoy them. However, with such youngsters, their ultimate quality is harder to assess.
2. Chances are improved if a kitten has already won awards

THE BREEDING PROCESS

Sexual maturity in cats may come as early as four months of age. Breeding should not be considered until the female is at least 12 months old, especially in the slow-maturing breeds such as those of Persian and European stock ancestry. A young cat barely out of her kitten stage may not have the required physical or psychological stability to produce and raise a vigorous litter. After her first heat, a female will normally come into heat again every two to three weeks and continue to do so until mated. The actual oestrous period lasts three to eight days. It is during this time that she is receptive to a male.

Once the mating has been successful, the time between fertilisation and birth of the young, known as the gestation period, is in the range of 59 to 67 days, 63 or 64 days being typical. The litter size will generally be two to five. Kittens are born blind and helpless, but develop rapidly. Their eyes open about the seventh day. By 21 days, they start exploring. At this time, they also will be sampling solid foods. By eight weeks, they can be vaccinated and neutered if required. Weaning normally commences by the age of six weeks and is completed within two to three weeks.

Kittens can go to a new home when 12 weeks old, though 14 to 16 weeks is preferred. During this period, you must decide if you wish to register the kittens or merely 'declare' them. This allows them to be registered at a later time. Obtain the necessary information and forms from your cat-registration authority. You should also consider the benefits of registering your own breeder prefix. This, however, is only worthwhile if you intend to breed on a more than casual basis. If you have decided that certain kittens are unsuitable for showing/breeding, do consider early neutering.

Breeders must determine which kittens in the litter will be show and/or breeding quality, and which ones will excel as companions.

Exhibiting Your
ABYSSINIAN CAT

EXAMPLES OF CLASSES AT SHOWS

Open	Cats of the specified breed.
Novice	Cats that have never won a first prize.
Limit	Cats that have not won more than first prizes.
Junior	Cats over nine months of age but less than two years on the day of the show.
Senior	Cats over two years old.
Visitors	Cats living a given distance away from the show venue.
Assessment	Experimental breeds, which have approved standards.
Aristocrat	Cats with one or two Challenge Certificates so are not yet full Champions (or Premiers for neuters).

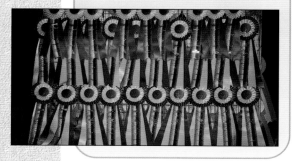

Without shows, the cat fancy could not exist. There would be only an handful of breeds as compared with today's ever-growing list. There would be fewer colour patterns and far less cat awareness. Given the great importance of shows to the cat fancy, it is perhaps a little surprising, and disappointing, that the majority of cat owners have never visited a feline exhibition.

Shows such as the National and the Supreme of Britain, or their equivalents in other countries, are the shop windows of the world of domestic cats. They are meeting places where breeders from all over the country compete to establish how well their breeding programmes are developing. A show also is a major social event on the cat calendar.

Whether a potential pet owner or breeder of the future, you should visit one or two shows. It is a great day out for the whole family. Apart from the wonderful selection of breeds, there are also many trade stands. If a product is available, it will be seen at the large exhibitions.

Many of the national clubs and magazines have stands. The

If you plan to show your Abyssinian, the extra expense and effort in acquiring top-quality representatives of the breed will pay off many times over.

two major shows mentioned are held in the winter months, usually November and December. However, there are hundreds of other shows staged during the year in various parts of the country. They range from small local club events to major championship breed shows and are usually advertised in the cat magazines. Your ruling cat association also can supply a list of shows.

SHOW ORGANISATION

So you will have some idea of how things are organised, the following information will be

ON THE CONTINENT AND BEYOND...

In Britain, the title of UK Grand Champion or Premier is won in competition with other Grand titleholders. In mainland Europe, cats can become International Champions. More British cats are expected to become International Champions with the recent introduction of passports for cats, allowing cats to compete more freely on the Continent and beyond. In countries other than Britain, the way in which shows are organised and titles achieved do differ somewhat. However, they broadly follow the outline discussed here.

There is, thus, the opportunity for every type of cat, from the best of Abyssinians to the everyday 'moggie' pets, to take part. These three broad categories are divided into various sections. For example, the unaltered and neuters are divided into their respective sections, such as Longhair, Semi-Longhair, British, Foreign, Siamese and so on.

There are many more classes other than those mentioned. These include club classes and those for kittens and non-pedigreed cats.

JUDGING

There are two ways cats can be judged. One is pen judging, the other is bench or ring judging. In

In addition to near-perfect conformation, the show-quality Abyssinian needs that extra twinkling 'something' to catch the eye of the judges.

helpful. You will learn even more by purchasing the show catalogue. This contains the names and addresses of the exhibitors and details of their cats. It also lists the prizes, indicates the show regulations and carries many interesting advertisements.

A major show revolves around three broad categories of cats:
1. Unaltered cats, meaning those that are capable of breeding.
2. Neuters.
3. Non-pedigreed cats.

CLASSES FOR NON-PEDIGREED CATS

For non-pedigreed cats, there are many classes, which include those for single colours, bicolours, tabbies, half-pedigreed, and so on. In this section, are many delightful classes, such as those for cats owned by pensioners, by young children (by age group), best original stray or rescued cat, best personality, most unusual-looking, most photogenic and best older cat. Within this cat section can be seen some truly gorgeous felines. There is no doubt that the pet classes have been the springboard that has launched many a top breeder into the world of pedigreed cats.

Britain, pen judging is the normal method, though bench judging is used for Best in Show. In pen judging, the judge moves around the cat pens. The cat gaining the most points when compared to the standard wins. In bench judging, stewards take the cats to the judge.

If a cat wins its class, it then competes against other class winners. By this process of elimination, a cat may go on to win the Best of Breed award. It then competes against other breed winners for the Best in Group award. The group winners then compete for the Best in Show award.

A breeder can gather a number of awards during the course of a show. Even those who do not own the very best cats can take pride in gaining second, third, fourth and recommended, especially if won at the larger shows. By progression, the top cat at a show will win its class, its breed and its section, and ultimately become the Best in Show exhibit. The titles a cat can win commence with that of Champion (or Premier in the case of neuters). A Grand Champion is made after winning in competition with others of its same status. The same applies to a Grand Premier. The judging system may vary from one country to another, but the basis remains as outlined.

BECOMING AN EXHIBITOR

Before any hobbyist enters a show, he is advised to join a local cat club. Here, hobbyists will meet local breeders who will not only assess their cats for them but also provide help on many other topics. The novice exhibitor could attend one or two shows with an exhibitor in order to learn the ropes. During this period, he can become familiar with the show rules and regulations. These are quite extensive, intended to safeguard the best interests of the hobby, the exhibitors and, most importantly, the cats.

It is of interest to note that some breeders own cats in partnership with other fanciers. This is useful when one person enjoys the breeding side and the other the exhibition side. It enables both really to be involved in the hobby to a level that might not have been possible for either on his own. So, whether you fancy being an exhibitor or you just love cats, do make a point of visiting the next major show in your area.

Abyssinians are highly regarded around the world and have been honoured with the title of Best Cat in Show at the most prestigious of shows. In the US, this red Aby won the CFA's show at Madison Square Garden in New York City in 1988.

An healthy, temperamentally sound cat shows no signs of fear or aggression, always appearing confident and self-possessed. This ruddy Aby believes he is the king of the jungle.

THE SHOW CAT

When a cat is seen preening in its pen, the hard work that has gone into its preparation is rarely appreciated. Exhibits must be in peak condition and their coats in full bloom. The potential exhibit must be trained gradually to spend hours within its show pen. It must display no fear or aggression towards strangers, such as the stewards or the judges. These must be able to examine the cat physically, including its ears and teeth; it also involves being lifted into the air. If a cat scratches or bites a judge, or any other show official, it is automatically withdrawn from the show. A repeat of this in the future would result, in most instances, in the cat's show career being terminated by the ruling association.

Apart from being comfort-able with people peering into its pen, the cat must be able to endure long journeys to the show venue. Unless trained, the cat may become a nervous, aggres-sive feline that will have a very short show career.

Obviously, the cat must display quality. This means having none of the major faults that would prevent it from gaining a first prize. These are listed in the breed standard. The meaning of quality is very subjective. You do not need to own a potential champion to be a successful exhibitor. The cat also must be registered with the association under whose rules the show is being run. In Britain, this will be the Governing Council of the Cat Fancy (GCCF) or The Cat Association of Britain.

As in anything competitive, exhibits can gain prizes at the lower levels of an hobby without having any realistic chance of awards in the major shows. Owning such exhibits is often part of a top breeder/exhibitor's portfolio from his early days in the hobby. Others may never move beyond the smaller shows but still gain reputations for owning sound stock. They thoroughly enjoy being involved at their given level.

If the idea of exhibiting appeals to you, the best way to make a start is to join a local club. There you not only will be advised on all procedures but also will be able to make many new friends. Exhibiting can be costly in cash and time, but you can focus on the more local shows while attending the larger ones as a visitor.

Maintaining a cat in the peak of good health revolves around the implementation of a sound husbandry strategy. At the basic level, this means being responsible about feeding, cleanliness and grooming. However, in spite of an owner's best efforts in these matters, cats still may become ill due to other causes. Although owners can attempt to prevent, identify and react to problems, only a vet is qualified to diagnose and suggest and/or effect remedies. Attempts by owners or 'informed' friends to diagnose and treat specific diseases are dangerous and potentially life-threatening to the cat.

SELECTING A VETERINARY SURGEON

Your selection of a veterinary surgeon should be based upon his skills with small animals, especially cats, and his personality, as well as his convenience to your home. You want a vet who is close because you might have emergencies or need to make multiple visits for treatments. You want a vet who has services that you might require such as nail clipping and bathing, as well as sophisticated pet supplies and a good reputation for ability and responsiveness. There is nothing more frustrating than having to wait a day or more to get a response from your veterinary surgeon.

All veterinary surgeons are licenced and their diplomas and/or certificates should be displayed in their waiting rooms.

A LONG, HEALTHY LIFE

As veterinary surgeons make medical advances in the health care of cats, the longevity of the typical house cat is improving. Certainly ages between 15 and 18 years are not uncommon, and reports of cats living more than 20 years are predictable.

KEEPING YOUR CAT HEALTHY

Although there are a multitude of ailments, diseases and accidents that could befall a cat, all but the most minor of problems can be avoided with good management. The following tips are a recipe for keeping your cat in the peak of health.

- Make sure it is vaccinated and in other ways protected from each of the major diseases. It must also receive annual boosters to maintain immunity.
- Have periodic checks made by your vet to see if your cat has worms.
- Ensure that the cat receives an adequate diet that is both appealing and balanced.
- Have the kitten neutered if it is not to be used for breeding.
- Ensure that the cat's litter tray, food/water vessels and grooming tools are always maintained in spotless condition.
- Do not let your cat out overnight or when you are away from home.
- Always wash your hands after gardening or petting other people's pets.
- Groom your cat daily. If this is done, you will more readily notice fleas or other problems than if grooming were done less frequently.
- Never try to diagnose and treat problems that are clearly of an internal type. Remember, even the most informed of breeders is not a vet and unable to reliably diagnose problems for you or advise treatments. Contact your vet.
- If you are ever in doubt about the health of your cat, do not delay in discussing your concerns with your vet. Delays merely allow problems to become more established.

There are, however, many veterinary specialities that usually require further studies and internships. There are specialists in heart problems (veterinary cardiologists), skin problems (veterinary dermatologists), teeth and gum problems (veterinary dentists), eye problems (veterinary ophthalmologists) and x-rays (veterinary radiologists), as well as vets who have specialities in reproduction, nutrition and behaviour. Most veterinary surgeons do routine surgery, such as neutering and stitching up wounds. When the problem affecting your cat is serious, it is not unusual or impudent to get another medical opinion, although in Britain you are obliged to advise the vets concerned about this. You might also want to compare costs among several veterinary surgeons. Sophisticated health care and veterinary services can be very costly. It is not infrequent that important decisions are based upon financial considerations.

PREVENTATIVE MEDICINE

It is much easier, less costly and more effective to practise preventative medicine than to fight bouts of illness and disease. Properly bred kittens come from parents who were selected based upon their genetic disease profile. Their mothers should have been vaccinated, free of all internal and external parasites and properly nourished. For these reasons, a visit to the veterinary surgeon who cared for the queen is recommended. The queen can pass on disease resistance to her kittens, which can last for eight to ten weeks. She can also pass on parasites and many infections. That's why it is helpful to know about the queen's health.

VACCINATIONS

Most vaccinations are given by injection and only should be done by a veterinary surgeon. Both he and you should keep a record of the date of the injection, the identification of the vaccine and the amount given. The first vaccination normally is given when the kitten is about 8–9 weeks old. About 30 days later, a booster is given. Although there are many diseases to which a cat may fall victim, the most dangerous three—FIE, FVR and FeLV—can be safeguarded against with a single (three-in-one) injection. Thereafter, an annual booster is all that is required.

MAJOR DISEASES

There are a number of diseases for which there is either no cure or little chance of recovery. However, some can be prevented by vaccination. All breeders and owners should ensure kittens are so protected.

FELINE INFECTIOUS ENTERITIS (FIE)

This is also known as feline panleukopenia, feline distemper and feline parvovirus. The virus attacks the intestinal system. It is spread via the faeces and urine. The virus may survive for many

BLOOD GROUP INCOMPATIBILITY (BGI)

In recent years, blood group incompatibility has become the focus of scientists, vets and breeders. Its importance to pet owners is when transfusions are needed. For breeders, it probably accounts for a large percentage of kittens that die from fading kitten syndrome. Scientifically the problem is called neonatal erythrolysis, meaning the destruction of red blood cells in newly born offspring.

Cats have two blood groups, A & B. Group A is dominant to B (which is genetically called recessive). When the antibodies of group-B mothers are passed to group-A kittens, via her colostrum milk, they destroy red blood cells. Death normally follows within a few days.

Most domestic cats tested are group A. However, national and regional differences display a variation in which 1-6% may be of type B. In pedigree breeds, it has been found that the number of group B cats varies significantly. The following breeds, based on present available data, have the indicated percentage incidence of group B blood type.

0%	Siamese, Burmese and Oriental Shorthair
1-5%	Maine Coon, Manx and Norwegian Forest
10-20%	Abyssinian, Birman, Japanese Bobtail, Persian, Scottish Fold and Somali
25-50%	British Shorthair, Devon and Cornish Rex and Exotic Shorthair

The clear implication to breeders is to establish their cats' blood group, via testing, and conduct appropriate matings. These should not result in group-B mothers' nursing group-A kittens. The safe matings are:

1. Group-A males   x   A females
2. Group-B males   x   A or B females
3. Group-A females x   A or B males
4. Group-B females x   B males

Breeders are advised to seek further information before embarking on stock purchase and breeding programmes.

years in some environments. The use of household bleach (sodium hypochlorite) for cleaning helps to prevent colonisation. Signs, among others, are diarrhoea, vomiting, depression, anorexia and dehydration. Death may occur within days. A vaccine is available.

FELINE VIRAL RHINOTRACHEITIS (FVR) & FELINE CALCIVIRUS (FCV)
Also known as cat flu, this is a complex of upper respiratory diseases. Signs are excessively hard sneezing, runny nose and mouth ulcers. Cats vaccinated after having contracted flu may recover but may suffer from recurrent bouts, especially if they become stressed.

STRESS TEST

Stress reduces the effectiveness of the immune system. Seemingly innocuous conditions may develop into major problems or leave the cat more open to attack by disease. Stress is difficult to identify specifically, but its major causes are well known. These include incorrect diet, intrusion by another cat in its home or territory, excessive handling and petting, disturbed sleep, uncomfortable home temperatures, bullying by another cat or pet, parasitic infestation, boarding in a cattery, travel, moving, boredom, limited accommodation space and, for some felines, being exhibited.

HEALTH AND VACCINATION TIMETABLE

AGE	6 WKS	8 WKS	10 WKS	12 WKS	16 WKS	6 MOS	1 YR
Worm control	✔	✔	✔		✔		
Neutering						✔	
Rhinotracheitis	✔	✔		✔	✔		✔
Panleukopenia	✔	✔		✔			✔
Calcivirus		✔			✔		✔
Feline Leukaemia				✔			✔
Feline Infectious Peritonitis				✔	✔		✔
Faecal evaluation						✔	
Feline Immunodeficiency testing							✔
Feline Leukaemia testing				✔			✔
Dental evaluation		✔				✔	
Rabies				✔	✔		✔

Vaccinations are not instantly effective. It takes about two weeks for the cat's immune system to develop antibodies. Most vaccinations require annual booster shots. Your veterinary surgeon should guide you in this regard.

DISEASE REFERENCE CHART

	What is it?	Cause	Symptoms
Feline Leukaemia Virus (FeLV)	Infectious disease; kills more cats each year than any other feline infectious disease.	A virus spread through saliva, tears, urine and faeces of infected cats; bite wounds.	Early on no symptoms may occur, but eventually infected cats experience signs from depression and weight loss to respiratory distress. FeLV also suppresses immune system, making a cat susceptible to almost any severe chronic illness.
Rabies	Potentially deadly virus that infects warm-blooded mammals.	A bacterium, often carried by rodents, that enters through mucous membranes and spreads quickly throughout the body.	Aggressiveness, a blank or vacant look in the eyes, increased vocalisation and/or weak or wobbly gait.
Feline Infectious Enteritis (FIE) *aka Panleukopenia*	Highly contagious virus, potentially deadly.	Ingestion of the virus, which is usually spread through the faeces of infected cats.	Most common: severe diarrhoea. Also vomiting, fatigue, lack of appetite, severe inflammation of intestines.
Feline Viral Rhinotracheitis (FVR)	Viral disease that affects eyes and upper respiratory tracts.	A virus that can affect any cat, especially those in multiple-cat settings.	Sneezing attacks, coughing, drooling thick saliva, fever, watery eyes, ulcers of mouth, nose and eyes.
Feline Immunodeficiency Virus (FIV)	Virus that reduces white blood cells.	An infection spread commonly through cat-fight wounds.	Signs may be dormant for years or innocuous, such as diarrhoea or anaemia.
Feline Infectious Peritonitis (FIP)	A fatal viral disease, may be linked to FeLV and FIV.	Bacteria in dirty litter boxes; stress may increase susceptibility in kittens.	Extremely variable; range from abdominal swelling to chest problems, eye ailments and body lesions.
Feline Urological Syndrome (FUS)	A disease that affects the urinary tracts of cats.	Inflammation of bladder and urethra.	Constipation, constant licking of penis or vulva, blood in urine (males), swollen abdomen, crying when lifted.

CARE OF FELINE KIDNEYS

The kidney of the cat is larger than that of the dog, but it has the typical bean shape. It receives 25% of the blood output of the heart! For this reason, it has rather significant veins to accommodate this large supply of blood, and injuries suffered by the kidneys are usually serious and not uncommon.

FELINE LEUKAEMIA VIRUS (FELV)

This is an highly infectious viral disease. It is spread via direct contact—mutual grooming, saliva, tears, feeding bowls, faeces, urine and biting. It can be passed prenatally from a queen to her offspring. It creates tumours, anaemia, immune system depression, pyrexia (high temperatures), lethargy, respiratory disease, intestinal disease and many other potentially fatal problems. It is most prevalent in high-density cat populations. Not all cats will be affected, but they may become carriers.

Kittens less than six months old are especially vulnerable.

NEUTERING

Neutering is a major means of avoiding ill health. It dramatically reduces the risk of males' becoming involved in territorial battles with the dangers of physical injury and disease transference. It makes the male more placid and less likely to scent mark his home. It also reduces the incidence of prostate problems, and there is no risk of testicular cancer. The female avoids potentially lethal illnesses related to her being allowed to remain in an unmated condition, such as breast cancer.

Neutering is usually performed between four and six months of age, but it can be done as early as eight weeks of age. Data available on the age at which a kitten is neutered indicate that early neutering has more advantages than drawbacks. Breeders should have this performed on all cats sold as pets.

Male cats are neutered. The operation removes the testicles and requires that the cat be anaesthetised. Females are spayed. This is major surgery during which the ovaries and uterus are removed. Both males and females should be kept quiet at home for about seven to ten days following the procedure, at which time the vet will remove the sutures.

Infected cats usually die by the time they are three to four years old. Cats can be screened or tested for this disease. Vaccination is not 100% effective but is recommended in kittens being sold into multi-cat environments.

FELINE IMMUNODEFICIENCY VIRUS (FIV)

This causes the white blood cells to be significantly reduced, thus greatly suppressing the efficiency of the immune system. It is not transferable to humans. Infection is normally gained from cat-fight wounds; thus, outdoor males are at greater risk. A cat diagnosed via blood tests as FIV-positive may live a normal life for months or years if retained indoors and given careful attention. Signs may be innocuous in the early stages, such as anaemia or diarrhoea. No vaccine is available.

FELINE INFECTIOUS PERITONITIS (FIP)

This viral disease is invariably fatal once contracted in its more potent forms. However, the virulence of the virus is variable and may by destroyed by the immune system. Stress may increase susceptibility in kittens. It may be linked to FeLV and FIV. Signs are extremely variable and range from abdominal swelling to chest problems, eye ailments to body lesions. There are various tests available but none is as yet 100% conclusive. Strict cleanliness is essential, especially of litter trays. No vaccine is available.

FELINE UROLOGICAL SYNDROME (FUS)

This is a very distressing condition caused by an inflammation of the bladder and urethra. Signs are constipation-like squatting and attempts to urinate, regular licking of the penis or vulva, blood in urine (males), swollen abdomen, crying when lifted and urinating in unusual places (often in only small amounts).

The numerous causes include infection, dirty litter tray of the indoor cat, alkaline urine (in cats, it should be acidic), diet too dry, lack of water intake (even though this is available) and being hit by a vehicle (damaged nerves). Veterinary treatment is essential or the condition could be fatal due to the bladder's bursting or the presence of dangerous bacteria.

RABIES

Britain and most European Community countries are free of this terrible disease. The stringent quarantine laws of Britain are such that vaccination is not necessary. However, the introduction of passports for dogs and cats means that resident British cats must be vaccinated if they are to travel abroad and return to the UK without being placed into quarantine. The vaccination is given when the kitten is three or more months old. The pet passport process takes at least six months to complete, so plan well ahead.

COMMON HEALTH PROBLEMS

DERMATITIS (ECZEMA)

Dry, lifeless coat, loss of coat, tiny scabs over the head and body, loose flakes (dandruff) and excessive scratching are all commonly called eczema. The cause covers a range of possibilities including diet, parasitic mites such as *Cheyletiella spp*, fungus or an allergy to flea or other bites. Sometimes reasons are unknown. Veterinary diagnosis and treatment are required.

RINGWORM (DERMATOPHYTOSIS)

This problem is fungal, not that of a worm. The most common form is *Microsporum canis*, which accounts for over 90% of cases. Cats less than one year of age are at the highest risk, while longhaired breeds are more prone to the problem than shorthaired cats. The fungi feed on the keratin layers of the skin, nails and hair. Direct contact and spores that remain in the environment are the main means of transmission.

Typical signs are circular-type bald areas of skin, which may be flaked and reddish. The coat generally may become dry and

POSSIBLE SOURCES OF EAR PROBLEMS

- Fight scratches
- Excess secretion of wax
- Swellings and blood blisters (haematoma) resulting from intrusion by foreign bodies (grass, seeds, etc.)
- Sunburn
- Whitish coloured ear mites (*Otodectes cynotis*)
- Orange-coloured harvest mites (*Trombicula autumnalis*)
- Fleas
- Bacterial infection of either the outer or middle/inner ear

lifeless, giving the appearance of numerous other skin and hair problems. Veterinary diagnosis and treatment, either topical or via drugs, is essential as the condition are zoonotic, meaning that it can be transferred to humans.

EAR PROBLEMS

Most of the common ear problems affect the outer ear. The telltale sign is the cat's constant scratching of the ears and/or its holding the ear to one side. Greasy hairs around the ear, dark brown wax (cerumen) in the ears, scaly flakes in or around the ear and minute white or orange pinhead-like bodies (mites) in the ear are common signs. *Canker* is a term used for ear infections, but it has no specific meaning.

Over-the-counter remedies for ear problems are ineffective unless correct diagnosis has been made. It is therefore better to let the vet diagnose and treat the cat. Some serious problems may require anaesthesia and minor surgery.

DIARRHOEA

This is a general term used to indicate a semi-liquid to liquid state of faecal matter. Mild to acute cases may be due to a change of environment, dietary change, eating an 'off' item, gorging on a favoured food, stress or a minor chill. These often rectify themselves within days. Chronic and persistent diarrhoea may be the result of specific diseases. Any indication of blood in the faecal matter must be considered dangerous.

In minor cases, withholding food for 12–24 hours, or feeding a simple diet, may arrest the condition. If not, contact your vet;

faecal analysis and blood testing may be required. By answering numerous questions related to the cat's diet, general health, level of activity, loss of appetite, etc., the vet will determine whether tests are required or if immediate treatment is warranted. Do not give cats human or canine intestinal remedies; these could prove dangerous.

CONSTIPATION

When a cat strains but is unable to pass motions, this is indicative of various causes. It may have hairballs, may have eaten a bird or rodent and has a bone lodged in its intestinal tract, may be suffering from a urological problem rather than constipation, or may have been hit by a car and has damaged the nerves that control bowel movements. As constipation is potentially serious, veterinary advice should be sought. Laxatives and faecal softener tablets may be given, the faecal matter can be surgically removed or another treatment can be carried out.

HEALTHIER CATS

The enormous population of pet cats has stimulated the veterinary medical community to learn more about cats and to develop more modern medicines to keep felines healthier.

GINGIVITIS (Plasmocytic-Lymphocytic Stomatitis)

There are many causes of this condition, but the end result is the same—bad breath, excessive plaque, tooth loss and, almost certainly, pain. The cat salivates excessively, starts to eat less and consequently loses weight. On inspection, the gums are swollen, especially in the areas of the premolar and molar teeth. They bleed easily. There are various treatments, such as antibiotics, immunostimulants and disinfectant mouth gels. However, these invariably prove short-term and merely delay the inevitable treatment of extraction.

Prevention avoids this painful condition. Regular tooth inspection and cleaning, plus provision of hard-food items, such as cat biscuits, achieve this to a large extent. There are also special cat chews made of dried fish that help clean the teeth. They also contain antibacterial enzymes that minimise or prevent secondary bacteria from accumulating. Ask for these at your pet shop or vet's surgery. Gingivitis may commence in kittens, so do not think it is something that only occurs in older cats.

Whether allowed outdoors or kept indoors only, your Aby runs the risk of encounters with parasites, irritants, allergens and the like. Ensure your cat's health by consulting the vet at the first sign of any problems.

EXTERNAL PARASITES

FLEAS

Of all the problems to which cats are prone, none is more well known and frustrating than fleas. Indeed, flea-related problems are the principal cause of visits to veterinary surgeons. Flea infestation is relatively simple to cure but difficult to prevent. Periodic flea checks for your cat, conducted as well as annual health check-ups, are highly recommended. Consistent dosing with anthelmintic preparations is also advised. Parasites that are harboured inside the body are a bit more difficult to eradicate, but they are easier to control.

To control a flea infestation, you have to understand the flea's life cycle. Fleas are often thought of as a summertime problem but centrally heated homes have changed the life-cycle patterns, and fleas can be found at any time of the year. Fleas thrive in hot and humid environments; they soon die if the temperature drops below 2°C (35°F). The most effective method of flea control is a two-stage approach: one stage to kill the adult fleas and the other to control the development of pre-adult fleas. Unfortunately, no single active ingredient is effective against all stages of the life cycle.

Flea prevention is a challenge to cat owners in most places. This is an adult male flea.

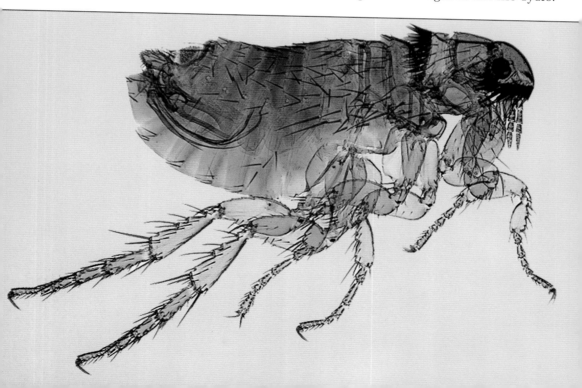

A Look at Fleas

Fleas have been around for millions of years and have adapted to changing host animals. They are able to go through a complete life cycle in less than one month, or they can extend their lives to almost two years by remaining as pupae or cocoons. They must have a blood meal every 10–14 days, and egg production begins within 2 days of their first meal. The female cat flea is very prolific and can lay 2000 eggs in her lifetime!

Fleas have been measured as being able to jump 300,000 times and can jump 150 times their body length in any direction, including straight up. Those are just a few of the reasons why they are so successful in infesting a cat!

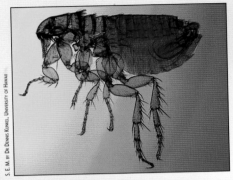

A scanning electron micrograph (S. E. M.) of a flea.

Magnified head of a flea.

LIFE CYCLE STAGES

During its life, a flea will pass through four life stages: egg, larva, pupa and adult. The adult stage is the most visible and irritating stage of the flea life cycle, and this is why the majority of flea-control products concentrate on this stage. The fact is that adult fleas account for only 1% of the total flea population, and the other 99% exist in pre-adult stages, i.e. eggs, larvae and pupae. The pre-adult stages are barely visible to the naked eye.

THE LIFE CYCLE OF THE FLEA

Eggs are laid on the cat, usually in quantities of about 20 or 30, several times a day. The female adult flea must have a blood meal before each egg-laying session. When first laid, the eggs will not cling to the cat's fur, as the eggs are not sticky. They will immediately fall to the floor or ground, especially when the cat moves around or scratches.

Once the eggs fall from the cat onto the carpet or grass, they will hatch into yellow larvae, approximately 2 mms long. This takes from 5 to 11 days. Larvae are not particularly mobile and will usually travel only a few inches from where they hatch. However, they do have a tendency to move away from light and heavy traffic—under furniture, in the carpet and behind doors are common places to find high quantities of flea larvae.

The flea larvae feed on dead organic matter, including adult flea faeces, until they are ready to change into adult fleas. Fleas will usually remain as larvae for around seven days, becoming darker in colour. After this period, the larvae will pupate a protective cocoon. While inside the pupae, the larvae will undergo metamorphosis and change into adult fleas. This can happen within a week, but the adult fleas can remain inside the pupae waiting to hatch for up to six months. The pupae are signalled to hatch by certain stimuli, such as physical pressure—the pupae's being stepped on, heat from an animal's lying on the pupae or increased

Opposite page: A scanning electron micrograph of a flea, magnified more than 100x. This image has been colorized for effect.

> **DO NOT MIX**
> Never mix flea-control products without first consulting your veterinary surgeon. Some products can become toxic when combined with others and can cause serious or fatal consequences.

> **FLEA-KILLER CAUTION**
> Flea killers are poisonous. You should not spray these toxic chemicals on areas of a cat's body that he licks, on his genitals or on his face. Flea killers taken internally are a better answer, but check with your vet in case internal therapy is not advised for your cat.

carbon dioxide levels and vibrations—indicating that a suitable host is available.

Once hatched, the adult flea must feed within a few days. Once the adult flea finds an host, it will not leave voluntarily. It only becomes dislodged by grooming or the host animal's scratching. The adult flea will remain on the host for the duration of its life unless forcibly removed.

TREATING THE ENVIRONMENT AND THE CAT
Treating fleas should be a two-pronged attack. First, the environment needs to be treated; this includes carpets and furniture, especially the cat's bedding and areas underneath furniture. The environment should be treated with an household spray containing an Insect Growth Regulator (IGR) and an insecticide to kill the adult fleas. There are also liquids, given orally, that contain chitin inhibitors. These

A brown tick, *Rhipicephalus sanguineus*, is an uncommon but annoying tick found on cats.

render flea eggs incapable of development. There are also both foam and liquid wipe-on treatments. Additionally, cats can be injected with treatments that can last up to six months. Emulsions that have the same effect can also be added to food. The advanced treatments are only available from veterinary surgeons.

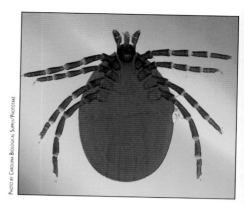

Photo by Carolina Biological Supply/Phototake

The IGRs actually mimic the fleas' own hormones and stop the eggs and larvae from developing into adult fleas. There are currently no treatments available to attack the pupa stage of the life cycle, so the adult insecticide is used to kill the newly hatched adult fleas before they find an host. Most IGRs are active for many months, while adult insecticides are only active for a few days.

The head of a tick, *Dermacentor variabilis*, enlarged and coloured for effect.

Photo by Dr Dennis Kunkel, University of Hawaii

When treating with an household spray, it is a good idea to vacuum before applying the product. This stimulates as many pupae as possible to hatch into adult fleas. The vacuum cleaner should also be treated with a flea

Dwight R Kuhn's magnificent action photo, showing a flea jumping.

treatment to prevent the eggs and larvae that have been hoovered into the vacuum bag from hatching.

The second stage of treatment is to apply an adult insecticide to the cat, usually in the form of a collar or a spray. Alternatively, there are drops that, when placed on the back of the cat's neck, spread throughout the fur and skin to kill adult fleas. A word of warning: Never use products sold for dogs on your cat; the result could be fatal.

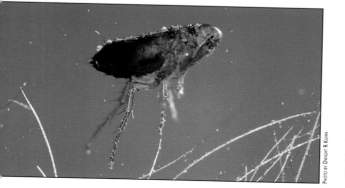

Photo by Dwight R Kuhn

The Life Cycle of the Flea

Eggs

Larvae

Pupa

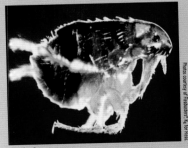

Adult

Photos courtesy of Frabustine® & for Fleas

Flea Control

IGR (INSECT GROWTH REGULATOR)

Two types of products should be used when treating fleas—a product to treat the pet and a product to treat the home. Adult fleas represent 1% of the flea population. The pre-adult fleas (i. e. eggs, larvae and pupae) represent 99% of the flea population and are found in the environment; it is in the case of pre-adult fleas that products containing an Insect Growth Regulator (IGR) should be used in the home.

IGRs are a new class of compounds used to prevent the development of insects. They do not kill the insect outright, but instead use the insect's biology against it to stop it from completing its growth. Products that contain methoprene are the world's first and leading IGRs. Used to control fleas and other insects, this type of IGR will stop flea larvae from developing and protect the house for up to seven months.

EN GARDE:
CATCHING FLEAS OFF GUARD!

Consider the following ways to arm yourself against fleas:

• Add a small amount of pennyroyal or eucalyptus oil to your cat's bath. These natural remedies repel fleas.
• Supplement your cat's food with fresh garlic (minced or grated) and an hearty amount of brewer's yeast, both of which ward off fleas.
• Use a flea comb on your cat daily. Submerge fleas in a cup of bleach to kill them quickly.
• Confine the cat to only a few rooms to limit the spread of fleas in the home.
• Vacuum daily...and get all of the crevices! Dispose of the bag every few days until the problem is under control.
• Wash your cat's bedding daily. Cover cushions where your cat sleeps with towels, and wash the towels often.

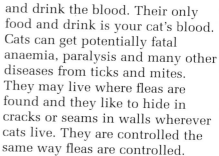

Opposite page: The tick, *Dermacentor variabilis*, is one of the most common ticks found on cats. Look at the strength in its eight legs! No wonder it's hard to detach them.

TICKS AND MITES

Though not as common as fleas, ticks and mites are found all over the tropical and temperate world. They don't bite like fleas; they harpoon. They dig their sharp proboscis (nose) into the cat's skin and drink the blood. Their only food and drink is your cat's blood. Cats can get potentially fatal anaemia, paralysis and many other diseases from ticks and mites. They may live where fleas are found and they like to hide in cracks or seams in walls wherever cats live. They are controlled the same way fleas are controlled.

The tick *Dermacentor variabilis* may well be the most common tick in many geographical areas, especially those areas where the climate is hot and humid. The other common ticks that attack small animals are *Rhipicephalus sanguineus, Ixodes* and some species of *Amblyomma*.

Most ticks have life expectancies of a week to six months, depending upon climatic conditions. They can neither jump nor fly, but they can crawl slowly and can range up to 5 metres (16 feet) to reach a sleeping or unsuspecting animal.

TOXOPLASMOSIS AND PREGNANT WOMEN

Toxoplasmosis is caused by a single parasite, *Toxoplasma gondii*. Cats acquire it by eating infected prey, such as rodents or birds, or raw meat. Obviously, strictly indoor cats are at less risk of infection than cats that are permitted to roam outdoors. Symptoms include diarrhoea, listlessness, pneumonia and inflammation of the eye. Sometimes there are no symptoms. The disease can be treated with antibiotics.

The only way humans can get the disease is through direct contact with the cat's faeces. People usually don't display any symptoms, although they can show mild flu-like symptoms. Once exposed, an antibody is produced and the person builds immunity to the disease.

The real danger to humans is that pregnant women can pass the parasite to the developing foetus. In this case, the chances are good that the baby will be born with a major health problem and/or serious birth defects. In order to eliminate risk, pregnant women should have someone else deal with the litter-box duties or wear gloves while taking care of the litter box and wash hands thoroughly afterwards.

INTERNAL PARASITES

Most animals—fishes, birds and mammals, including cats and humans—have worms and other parasites that live inside their bodies. According to Dr Herbert R Axelrod, the fish pathologist, there are two kinds of parasites: dumb and smart. The smart parasites live in peaceful cooperation with their hosts (symbiosis), while the dumb parasites kill their hosts. Most of the worm infections are relatively

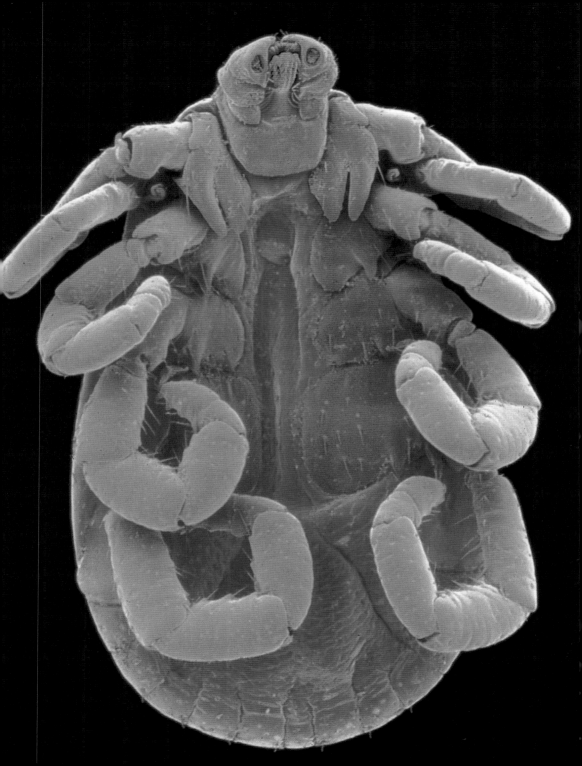

easy to control. If they are not controlled, they weaken the host cat to the point that other medical problems occur, but they are not dumb parasites.

HOOKWORMS

The worm *Ancylostoma tubaeforme* can infect a cat by the larva's penetrating the cat's skin. It attaches itself to the small intestine of the cat, where it sucks blood. This loss of blood could cause iron-deficiency anaemia.

Outdoor cats that spend much of their time in the garden or in contact with soil are commonly infected with hookworm. There is another worm, the *Gordius* or horsehair worm, that, if ingested by a cat, causes vomiting.

TAPEWORMS

There are many species of tapeworms. They are carried by

DEWORMING
Ridding your kitten of worms is VERY IMPORTANT because certain worms that kittens carry, such as tapeworms and roundworms, can infect humans.

Breeders initiate a deworming programme at or about four weeks of age. The routine is repeated every two or three weeks until the kitten is three months old. The breeder from whom you obtained your kitten should provide you with the complete details of the deworming programme.

Your veterinary surgeon can prescribe and monitor the programme of deworming for you. The usual programme is treating the kitten every 15–20 days until the kitten is positively worm-free. It is advised that you only treat your kitten with drugs that are recommended professionally.

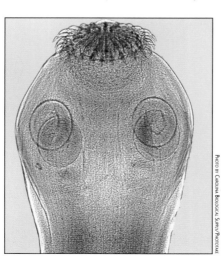

The head and rostellum (the round prominence on the scolex) of a tapeworm, which infects cats and humans.

PHOTO BY CAROLINA BIOLOGICAL SUPPLY/PHOTOTAKE

fleas! The cat eats the flea and starts the tapeworm cycle. Humans can also be infected with tapeworms, so don't eat fleas! Fleas are so small that your cat could pass them onto your hands, your plate or your food and thus make it possible for you to ingest a flea that is carrying tapeworm eggs.

While tapeworm infection is not life-threatening in cats (smart parasite!), it can be the cause of a

INTERNAL PARASITES OF CATS

NAME	DESCRIPTION	SYMPTOMS	ACQUISITION	TREATMENT
Roundworm (*Toxocara cati* and *Toxascaris leonina*)	Large, white, coil-like worms, 5–10 cms (2–4 inches) long, resembling small springs.	Vomiting, pot belly, respiratory problems, poor growth rate, protruding third eyelids, poor haircoat.	Ingesting infective larvae; ingesting infected mammals, birds or insects; a queen with *Toxocari cati* nursing kittens.	Anthelmintics; scrupulously clean environment (e.g. daily removal of all faeces recommended).
***Physaloptera* species**	2–15 cms (1–6 inches) long, attacks the wall of the stomach.	Vomiting, anorexia, melena.	Eating insects that live in soil (e.g. May beetles).	Diagnosed with a gastroscope; treated with pyrantel pamoate. Prevention of exposure to the intermediate hosts.
***Gordius* or Horsehair worm**	15-cm (6-inch) pale brown worms with stripes.	Vomiting.	May ingest a worm while drinking from or making contact with swimming pools and toilet bowls.	Anthelmintics; avoiding potentially infected environments.
Hookworm (*Ancylostoma tubaeforme*)	The adult worms, ranging from 6 to 15 mms (2.5–6 inches) in length, attach themselves to the small intestines.	Anaemia, melena, weight loss, poor haircoat.	Larva penetrating the cat's skin, usually attacks the small intestine. Found in soil and flower gardens where faecal matter is deposited.	Fortnightly treatment with anthelmintics. Good sanitation (e.g. daily cleanup of litter boxes).
Tapeworm (*Dipylidium caninum* and *Taenia taeniformis*)	Up to 91 cms (3 feet) long. Parts shaped similar to cucumber seeds. The most common intermediate hosts are fleas and biting lice.	No clinical signs—difficult to detect.	Eating infected adult fleas. Uses rodents as hosts.	Praziquantel and epsiprantel. Management of environment to ensure scrupulously clean conditions. Proper flea control.

Magnified heartworm larvae, *Dirofilaria immitis*.

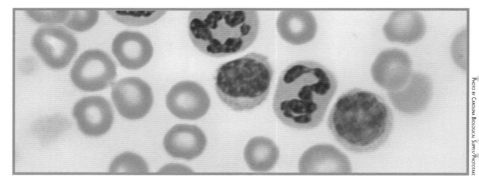

The heartworm, *Dirofilaria immitis*.

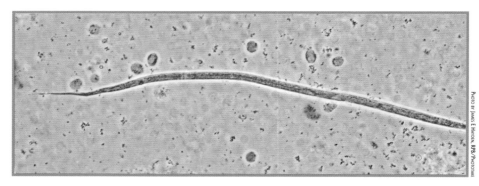

very serious liver disease for humans. About 50% of the humans infected with *Echinococcus multilocularis*, a type of tapeworm that causes alveolar hydatis, perish.

HEARTWORMS
Heartworms are thin, extended worms up to 30 cms (12 ins) long, which are difficult to diagnose in cats as the worms are too few to be identified by the antigen-detection test. Symptoms may be loss of energy, loss of appetite, coughing, the development of a potbelly and anaemia. Heartworm infection in cats should be treated very seriously, as it is often fatal.

Heartworms are transmitted by mosquitoes. The mosquito drinks the blood of an infected cat and takes in larvae with the blood. It takes two to three weeks for the larvae to develop to the infective stage within the body of the mosquito. Cats are less frequently infected with heartworms than are dogs. Also, the parasite is more likely to attack the cat's brain or other organs rather than the heart. Cats should be treated at about six weeks of age and maintained on a prophylactic dose given monthly.

THE FELINE EYE

by Lorraine Waters BvetNed, CertVOphthal, MRCVS

This part of the book aims to provide an owner's guide to feline ophthalmology, the study of eyes, which is an area of increasing concern for cat owners.

Eye diseases in the cat usually result from trauma, infection or neoplasia (cancer). Unlike the dog, the cat has few inherited eye conditions. Most of the conditions to be discussed are not amenable to first-aid measures or home remedies. Therefore, if you are at all worried about your cat's eyes, you should seek prompt veterinary attention.

Ocular pain is frequently associated with eye disease and can be recognised in your cat because it will show a combination of the following signs:
blinking, increased tear production, fear of light and rubbing at the eye. Some conditions result in loss of vision; a gradual loss of vision may go unnoticed, as the cat slowly adapts, but a sudden loss produces an obvious change in behaviour. Being blind may not be as bad as it sounds, as cats adapt and cope amazingly well in familiar surroundings.

To examine the eye properly, veterinary surgeons first use a bright light, which allows close examination of the lids, conjunctiva, cornea and iris. Following this, an ophthalmoscope can be used, in a darkened room, to give a magnified view. Then, by using the lenses within the ophthalmoscope, it is possible to focus on the structures further back in the eye, such as the lens, vitreous and retina.

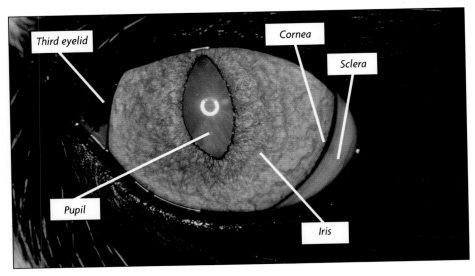

Third eyelid · Cornea · Sclera · Pupil · Iris

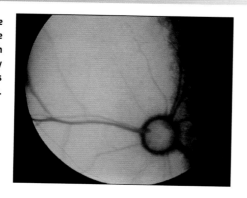

The feline fundus, the eye as seen through the veterinary surgeon's ophthalmoscope.

DISEASES OF THE FELINE EYE

GLOBE AND ORBIT

The eye sits in a bony socket in the skull known as the orbit. In short-nosed breeds, the orbit is shallow and the normal-sized eyes bulge forward. This situation can predispose a number of problems, such as exposure keratitis, overflow of tears and even prolapse of the globe (eye). Cats can be born with eyes that are too small and sink back into the orbit, to be covered by the third eyelid. This is non-inherited and usually associated with damage to the eye in utero. Abnormal enlargement of the globe may be congenital, buphthalmos, or acquired, hydrophthalmos, and is the end point of glaucoma.

The globe can prolapse from the orbit following head trauma, a common injury for cats involved in road-traffic accidents. A minor prolapse replaced early can result in restoration of normal function. However, there is often stretching of the optic nerve and tearing of the extra-ocular muscles. In these cases, the eye may be permanently damaged and have to be surgically removed. As an emergency measure, applying a moist cloth to the prolapsed eye on the way to the surgery will help preserve it.

Problems behind the eye become evident when they cause the eye to bulge forward along with the third eyelid. These include tooth root abscesses, foreign bodies, tumours and occasionally haemorrhages.

EYELIDS

The eyes of a kitten should open around 10–14 days of age. Once this has occurred, it is possible to see if the lids have been properly formed. Failure of all or part of the eyelids to develop is a rare congenital problem, known as coloboma.

EYE DROPS

Topical ointments and drops are often prescribed for the treatment of eye disease. There are a few simple rules to follow when administering them. It is important to clean away discharges before applying treatment. Only give one drop or just a few millilitres of ointment; if you give too much, it will be diluted by increased tear production. Systemic drugs are those given by mouth to achieve higher concentrations at the back of the eye or for diseases which involve other body systems.

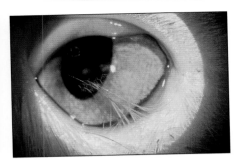

The unprotected cornea, in the affected area, may become damaged and the lid must be surgically restored. Early infection in the eye may delay or prevent the eyelid's opening; the lids can be opened surgically to allow bathing and appropriate medication to be given.

Entropion and ectropion are common conditions in the dog and are related to conformation. Fortunately, these are rare in cats and can be surgically corrected. Entropion secondary to ocular pain may remain once the cause of the pain is removed. Fortunately, these cases will respond to corrective surgery. Extra or abnormally positioned hairs are frequently seen as an inherited problem in dogs, but are rare in cats.

There are several types of tumours that can occur on the eyelids. The most common type is squamous cell carcinoma, more prevalent in white and part-white cats, as ultra-violet light (sunlight) plays a role in causing this condition. Treatment may consist of cryotherapy, surgical excision or radiation treatment. Early recognition and treatment are essential to prevent destructive local spreading.

CONJUNCTIVA

The pink tissue lining the eyelid and covering the third eyelid and front of the sclera is called conjunctiva. Dermoids are elements of skin tissue that arise in abnormal places. Dermoids often, but not invariably, contain hairs and can form on the conjunctiva and/or cornea. Dermoids act as foreign bodies in the eye, causing irritation and pain, and need to be surgically removed.

The most frequently encountered problem with the conjunctiva is conjunctivitis. In cats, the majority of cases are infectious. An eye with conjunctivitis usually looks red and swollen with signs of ocular pain. Discharges may be watery or sticky yellow, indicating bacterial infection.

The most common infectious cause of feline conjunctivitis is feline herpesvirus (FHV). Feline calicivirus (FCV) can also cause conjunctivitis and is usually

Eyelid coloboma is a rare congenital problem in cats.

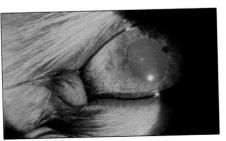

Dermoid in a longhaired cat.

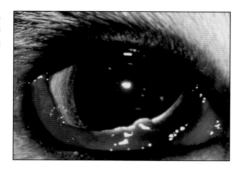

Conjunctivitis, frequently an infectious disease in cats.

Corneal ulcer stained with fluorescein.

associated with other problems, such as upper respiratory tract signs and mouth ulcers. The bacteria *Chlamydia psittaci* can cause conjunctivitis in individual cats and in multi-cat households. Individual cases respond well to appropriate antibiotic therapy. Chronic and recurrent conjunctivitis in multi-cat situations requires thorough and prolonged treatment, management changes and, where appropriate, vaccination. *Mycoplasma spp.* can cause a less severe conjunctivitis than *Chlamydia spp.* Opportunistic infection can occur following cat-fight wounds, as bacteria are found on cats' teeth and claws.

Non-infectious causes of

conjunctivitis include trauma, foreign bodies, allergic disease, tumours and pre-corneal tear film abnormalities. Eosinophilic kerato-conjunctivitis is a disease in which the conjunctiva and cornea are invaded by cells from the immune system, primarily mast cells and eosinophils. These cells are responsible for inflammation and allergic reactions. This tends to occur in young to middle-aged cats and may be seasonal. Treatment usually

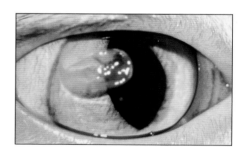

works well but may be required long-term.

Several forms of neoplasia can affect the conjunctiva in cats and can be either primary tumours arising in the conjunctiva or secondary, spreading from elsewhere in the body.

SCLERA

The sclera is the white fibrous coat of the globe. It is partially covered by conjunctiva and protects the more fragile internal structures. Congenital defects of this structure are very rare. Inflammation (scleritis and episcleritis) is a

Tear staining is more commonly seen in short-nosed cat breeds.

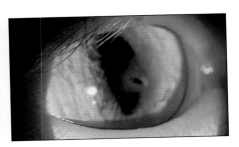

problem in dogs and humans but is extremely rare in cats. Feline scleral diseases are usually associated with trauma and cancer.

PRE-CORNEAL TEAR FILM

This forms from tears and moistens, lubricates and helps protect the cornea. Decreased tear production occurs if the tear glands are not working properly and results in a condition called 'dry eye' or keratoconjunctivis sicca (KCS). The cornea becomes dry and roughened, leading to keratitis and ulceration. It can occur following feline herpesvirus (FHV) infection, trauma, facial paralysis and chronic inflammation.

Overproduction of tears can be seen as a result of ocular pain. The naso-lacrimal duct drains the tears; it runs from the inner corner of the eye to just inside the end of the nose. Congenital defects, such as a small duct opening, result in tear overflow and staining around the eye. These usually can be corrected surgically. Acquired blockages may result from chronic conjunctivitis or foreign bodies.

Tear staining is also seen in short-nosed breeds because the duct is tortuous and drainage inadequate. This is also associated with medial lower lid entropion, occluding the duct opening. This anatomical combination is very difficult to improve surgically.

Corneal foreign body.

CORNEA

The cornea is the clear circular area at the front of the eye through which the iris and pupil can be seen. Light passes through and is focused by the cornea, before passing through the lens and hence onto the retina. Congenital defects are rare but include micro- and megalocornea. There is sometimes a transient cloudiness following the kitten's opening of the eyes, but it should disappear by four weeks of age.

One of the most common problems involving the cornea is ulceration, where the top layer of corneal cells (the epithelium) is lost and the nerve endings exposed, resulting in ocular pain. Fluorescein is a special stain that can be used to reveal ulcers; they

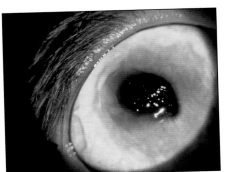

Corneal sequestrum.

Symblepharon, adhesion of the eyelid to the eyeball.

show up as a yellow-green patch on the cornea. If your cat has had this performed, you may have noticed the stain appearing at the end of its nose; this is because it drains down the naso-lacrimal duct and demonstrates that it is not blocked.

The most common cause of ulceration is·trauma, from fight wounds or foreign bodies. FHV can cause ulceration. There is also a form of ulceration where the epithelium does not stick down again after healing and can easily become detached. This is seen as a breed-related problem in dogs. In cats, it can be seen in older animals or associated with FHV infection, resulting in recurrent ulcer formation.

The cornea is very quick to repair ulcers and, provided that the initial cause is removed, healing should only take a few days. Antibiotics are often applied to the eye while ulcers heal to prevent bacterial infection. Ulcers need prompt veterinary attention as they can deteriorate rapidly; deep ulcers can lead to rupture of the eye and require urgent surgical repair.

The cornea is a common site for cat-scratch injuries and some may even penetrate the full thickness into the anterior chamber. If these wounds are repaired quickly and appropriate medical therapy is used, vision can usually be preserved. More severe ones may require reconstructive surgery, removal of the lens or even surgical removal of the eye.

Corneal foreign bodies usually result in ocular pain and need to be removed. Non-painful ones also need to be removed as they may penetrate the eye, causing internal problems.

Corneal sequestrum or necrosis is a condition specific to cats. The corneal stroma (middle layer) degenerates, turns brown/black and emerges through the epithelium, causing ulceration and a foreign body reaction with signs of ocular pain. These lesions usually need to be removed surgically because of the discomfort they cause, but a few will slough off naturally. Often a sequestrum will recur in the same eye or occur in the opposite eye at a later date. This condition is most commonly seen in Colourpoint Persians and is thought to have an inherited component. It may be related to their prominent eye position.

Following healing of a corneal wound, there is usually formation of a scar, which shows up as a white mark, but unless scars are extensive, they do not usually affect vision.

FHV-related Eye Diseases

A combination of treatments is often required to treat feline herpesvirus (FHV) infection. In acute cases, kittens are often very sick and need supportive treatment and intensive nursing. Systemic and topical antibiotics are used, sometimes in combination with topical antiviral drugs. Cats that develop symblepharon after acute infection may be blinded by the condition and require new reconstructive surgical techniques. The chronic cases can be difficult to diagnose and challenging to treat. Topical antivirals can be used and in non-ulcerated cases combined with corticosteroids. More recent treatments include L-lysine (to inhibit viral replication), Cimetidine and alpha-interferon (to boost the local immune response).

The reason for chronic FHV disease is that individuals become carriers of the virus. When they are stressed, the virus is reactivated and signs of infection and the cat's immune response to it manifest in the eye. This can be a major problem in multi-cat households, with carrier animals infecting kittens and adults alike. In these cases, management changes, including the identification of carriers, use of early vaccinations and isolation of new arrivals, must be instituted.

Aqueous Humour

The aqueous humour is a watery fluid that is responsible for maintaining pressure within the eye. If the drainage angle is blocked and aqueous cannot drain away, pressure within the eye builds up, causing glaucoma. Glaucoma due to a congenitally obstructed drainage system is an inherited problem in many breeds of dog but is rare in the cat. When glaucoma does occur in cats, it is usually acquired, with drainage blocked by inflammatory or neoplastic cells.

Anterior uveitis can result in white blood cells in the anterior chamber, which gives it a cloudy look known as aqueous flare. Infection following penetrating wounds can result in pus accumulating in the chamber, known as hypopyon. Trauma to the eye and intra-ocular tumours may lead to bleeding into the anterior chamber (space behind the cornea and in front of the iris), known as hyphaema. This blood usually

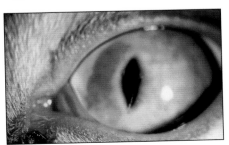

Herpesvirus ulcer.

forms a clot and is absorbed.
Foreign bodies also occasionally
can be seen in the anterior
chamber.

IRIS AND CILIARY BODY
The iris and ciliary body are
muscular and vascular structures
that lie behind the cornea and in
front of the lens. The iris is
pigmented and gives the cat's eye
its colour. Congenital defects are
rare, but occasionally cats are born
with pieces of the iris missing.
Changes in iris colour can occur for
a number of reasons; as young cats
mature, their iris colour may
deepen. Inflammation results in
reddening of the iris, due to an
increase in blood vessel formation
and engorgement, and is known as
rubeosis iridis. Following inflammation, the iris can remain
permanently dark.

As cats age, they can develop a
condition called melanosis. This is
usually but not always a diffuse
change, occurring slowly in both
eyes. It must be monitored and
differentiated from iris melanoma.

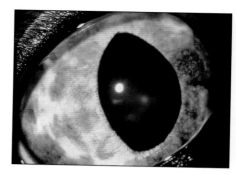

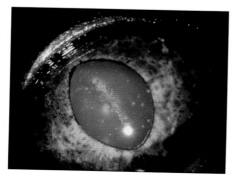

Melanoma is a tumour of the
pigment cells that can result in
either diffuse or nodular discol-
oration of the iris. It usually
progresses quickly and only in one
eye. This type of neoplasia has a
potential to spread outside the eye
and is usually treated by surgically
removing the affected eye.

A difference in colour between
the two irises is known as hetero-
chromia iridis and can occur
naturally in white or poorly
pigmented breeds, usually associated with congenital deafness. In
other cats, it usually indicates a
problem in one eye or the other.

The ciliary body and iris are
known as the anterior uvea, while
the choroid (the vascular layer that
lies between the retina and the
sclera and provides a blood supply
to the retina) is the posterior uvea.
Uveitis is an inflammation of the
uvea. It may involve both the
anterior and posterior uvea and has
many causes in the cat. The main
infectious causes are feline
immunodeficiency virus (FIV),
feline leukaemia virus (FeLV),

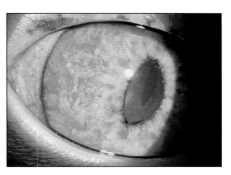

Uveitis, inflammation of the iris, ciliary body and choroid.

front. They are not neoplastic and do not usually need to be removed.

LENS

The lens is the clear disc-shaped structure suspended behind the iris, responsible for focusing light onto the retina. A cataract, or opacity of the lens and/or its capsule, is a disorder of the lens. Many forms of hereditary cataracts are seen in dogs but not in cats. Congenital cataracts are occasionally found as a non-inherited problem. Most of the cataracts seen in cats are formed secondary to lens damage, e.g. blunt trauma, penetrating wounds, chronic anterior uveitis and lens luxation. If cataracts involve the whole lens, light will not be able to get through to the retina and the eye will be rendered blind. If appropriate, cataracts can be surgically removed.

feline infectious peritonitis (FIP) and toxoplasmosis. Tuberculosis has been reported in cats as a cause of uveitis and, in sub-tropical and tropical countries, fungal infection can be a significant cause. The signs of uveitis for all of these diseases are very similar and may include a constricted pupil, rubeosis iridis, aqueous flare, poor vision and ocular pain. It can be difficult to determine the cause in some cases despite thorough investigation. Even if the primary viral infection cannot be cured, cats with uveitis can be treated symptomatically to ease discomfort and maintain vision. Long-term uveitis can lead to cataract formation, lens luxation and glaucoma. Non-infectious causes of uveitis include trauma and neoplasia.

If the lens's suspensory fibres weaken or break, it will become dislocated and can fall either into the back or front of the eye. This is a common breed-related problem in terrier dogs and is occasionally seen in cats, usually as a result of

Atrophy of the iris may occur as a result of ageing or following inflammation. Cysts of the iris are sometimes seen and look like tiny black balloons. They form on the back of the iris but can detach and float through the pupil to rest in

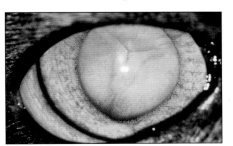

Cataract developed from long-term uveitis.

trauma, ageing or cataract. The lens usually is surgically removed to prevent it from blocking the pupil, which can lead to glaucoma.

The lens condenses with age, giving it a grey appearance, known as senile sclerosis. This is not a true cataract, as light can still pass through to the back of the eye and vision is not impaired.

One rare but important condition of the lens in the cat is post-traumatic sarcoma. If the lens is damaged by trauma, it can become neoplastic and rapidly fill the eye with tumours. Appropriate treatment at the time of the initial injury should prevent this, but when it does occur, surgical removal of the eye is recommended.

VITREOUS HUMOUR

The vitreous humour is a jelly-like substance that fills the space between the back of the lens and the front of the retina. Like the aqueous humour, the vitreous can be infiltrated with haemorrhage and inflammatory cells. Foreign bodies can occasionally be found in the vitreous. Inflammation of the vitreous, known as hyalitis, can be seen as part of generalised uveitis.

The vitreous humour degenerates with age, giving a cloudy appearance to the back of the eye, but this does not usually affect vision to any great extent.

THINGS TO LOOK OUT FOR

A change in appearance of the eye
- Redness
- Cloudiness
- Change in iris colour

Increase in discharges
- Watery

Sticky mucoid
- Yellow
- Bloody

Blinking, squinting and head shyness
Aversion to light
Rubbing at the eye
Loss of vision
Protrusion of the eye
Loss of facial symmetry

RETINA

The retina, at the back of the eye, is where the visual image is formed. Congenital retinal problems are rare in cats, but colobomas (defects or holes) can occasionally be seen in the optic disc (the point at which nerves converge to leave the eye as the optic nerve). Inflammation of the retina usually occurs together with inflammation of the choroid and is called chorioretinitis or posterior uveitis. The causes are the same as those for anterior uveitis. Inflammation can lead to retinal detachment, haemorrhage, degeneration and scarring of the retina. It can be difficult to diagnose the cause of posterior uveitis; thus, symptomatic treatment is generally given to

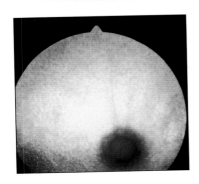

maintain vision.

The retina may also degenerate as a result of non-inflammatory processes. An inherited form of retinal degeneration has been described in the Abyssinian and Siamese breeds. Deficiency in dietary taurine (an amino acid) causes retinal degeneration. Fortunately, this is now rare as many commercial cat foods are supplemented with this compound. It may, however, still be a problem with some home-prepared diets.

Hypertension is a common cause of retinal disease in elderly cats. It may be primary, essential hypertension or secondary to other diseases, such as kidney disease, hyperthyroidism and diabetes. Hypertension causes changes in the retinal arteries, retinal and vitreal haemorrhages, retinal detachment and hyphaema. Early recognition and treatment are essential to prevent permanent ocular damage and damage to other organs, such as the kidney,

heart and brain.

Retinal detachment causes blindness and may result from hypertension, inflammation and neoplasia. If the retina does not reattach in 24–48 hours, there will be permanent vision loss. Symptomatic treatment is often given to reattach the retina, but it is also important to treat the underlying cause.

Retinal haemorrhages can occur as a result of hypertension, inflammation and trauma. They can cause temporary loss of vision but will often be resorbed. Once again, it is important to find the underlying cause and treat it accordingly without delay.

Finally, if in any doubt regarding the condition of your cat's eyes, it is always worthwhile consulting your veterinary surgeon. Even if you consider the condition to be minor, it may not remain so!

Advanced retinal degeneration.

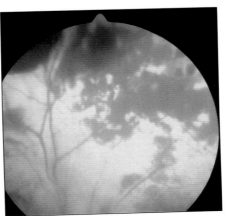

Retinal haemorrhages as a result of hypertension.

The author is grateful to the Animal Health Trust (England) for the illustrations used in the eye-health section

USEFUL ADDRESSES

GREAT BRITAIN
The Governing Council of the Cat Fancy (GCCF)
4-6 Penel Orlieu, Bridgwater, Somerset, TA6 3PG
Email: GCCF_CATS@compuserve.com Fax: 01278 446627 Tel: 01278 427575

The Cat Association of Britain
Mill House, Letcombe Regis, Oxon OX12 9JD   Tel: 01235 766543

EUROPE
Federation Internationale Feline (FIFe)
Gen. Sec: Ms Penelope Bydlinski
Little Dene, Lenham Heath, Maidstone, Kent ME17 2BS, GB
Email: penbyd@compuserve.com   Fax: 1622 850193 Tel: 1622 850908

World Cat Federation
Hubertsrabe 280, D-45307, Essen, Germany
Email: wcf@nrw-online.de   Fax: 201-552747 Tel: 201-555724

AUSTRALIA
The Australian Cat Federation, Inc.
PO Box 3305, Port Adelaide, SA 5015
Email: acf@catlover.com   Fax: 08 8242 2767 Tel: 08 8449 5880

CANADA
Canadian Cat Association (CCA)
220 Advance Boulevard, Suite 101, Brampton, Ontario L6T 4J5
Email: office@cca-afc.com   Fax: 99050 459-4023 Tel: 99060 459-1481

SOUTH AFRICA
Cat Federation of Southern Africa
PO Box 25, Bromhof 2154, Gauteng Province, Republic of South Africa

USA
American Cat Association (ACA)
8101 Katherine Avenue, Panorama City, CA 91402
Fax: (818) 781-5340 Tel: (818) 781-5656

American Cat Fanciers Association (ACFA)
PO Box 203, Point Lookout, MO 65726
Email: info@acfacat.com   Fax: (417) 334-5540 Tel: (417) 334-5430

Cat Fanciers Association, Inc. (CFA)
PO Box 1005, Manasquan, NJ 08736-0805
Email: cfa@cfainc.org   Fax: (732) 528-7391 Tel: (732) 528-9797

Cat Fanciers Federation (CFF)
PO Box 661, Gratis, OH 45330
Email: Lalbert933@aol.com Fax: (937) 787-4290 Tel: (937) 787-9009

The International Cat Association (TICA)
PO Box 2684, Harlingen, TX 78551
Email: ticaeo@xanadu2.net Tel: (956) 428-8046